Dead Men
of the
Fifties

ALSO BY PIER GIORGIO DI CICCO

We Are the Light Turning (1975, revised 1976)
The Sad Facts (1977)
The Circular Dark (1977)
Dancing in the House of Cards (1977)
A Burning Patience (1978)
Dolce-Amaro (1978)
The Tough Romance (1979, 1990)
translated as *Les Amour Difficiles* (1990)
A Straw Hat for Everything (1981)
Flying Deeper into the Century (1982)
Dark to Light: Reasons for Humanness, Poems 1976 – 1979 (1983)
Women We Never See Again (1984)
Post-Sixties Nocturne (1985)
Virgin Science: Hunting Holistic Paradigms (1986)
Living in Paradise—New and Selected Poems (2001)
The Honeymoon Wilderness (2002)
The Dark Time of Angels (2003)

AS EDITOR
Roman Candles: An Anthology of Seventeen Italo-Canadian Poets (1978)

Dead Men
of the
Fifties

Pier
Giorgio
Di Cicco

Mansfield Press

Copyright © Pier Giorgio Di Cicco 2004
All Rights Reserved
Printed in Canada

Library and Archives Canada Cataloguing in Publication

Di Cicco, Pier Giorgio, 1949 –
    Dead men of the Fifties / Pier Giorgio Di Cicco.

Poems.
ISBN 1-894469-19-4

I. Title.

PS8557.I248D43 2004   C811'.54   C2004-906291-3

Cover Design: Denis De Klerck
Interior Design: Marijke Friesen
Cover Photo: © Pierre Vauthey/Corbis Sygma/Magma

The publication of *Dead Men of the Fifties*
has been generously supported by
The Canada Council for the Arts and
The Ontario Arts Council.

Mansfield Press Inc.
25 Mansfield Avenue, Toronto, Ontario, Canada M6J 2A9
Publisher: Denis De Klerck
www.mansfieldpress.net

To those of 1946 – 1959

Table of Contents

Sweeney at the Chesapeake Lounge _ 1
How to Receive Signals _ 3
What an Adult Would Watch _ 4
Sweeney _ 7
A Picture Book of Baltimore _ 8
Remember _ 10
The Purely Personal _ 11
Pimlico _ 12
Sweeney at the Chesapeake Lounge _ 13
Seduction Song _ 14
Shore Leave _ 15
Maggie on the Dotted Line _ 16
Nite-Life _ 17
Meeting the Challenges of a Changing World _ 18
Sweeney Would Have Liked Route 66 _ 19
Smiley Burnette _ 20
Burlesque Queen _ 21
The Music Scene, 1947 _ 22
Of Sweeney _ 23
And So We Sing the Musics _ 24
Voices Wafting Through the Severna Park Marina _ 25
A Date With Sweeney _ 26
Pining _ 27
Dirge for Sidney _ 28
Johnson _ 29
The Men of Jazz _ 30
Bongo Intro _ 31
The Jive Pigs _ 32
The Future from Grant Street _ 33
Elegy for a Drummer _ 34
Katie and John _ 35
Sweeney's Ghost Speaks To Me _ 36
Round Again Record _ 37

Cavalcade _ 39
Weather and the Fifties _ 41
The Redheaded Widow _ 42
The Bow of the Missouri _ 43
On the North Atlantic _ 44
The Armistice Day Matinee _ 45
Back from Bellevue Psychiatric Hospital, 1951 _ 46
Spinster Set _ 47
We Ran Together in the Rain _ 48
What is the Nature of the Dead Men of the Fifties _ 49
Barfly, Jack Arema _ 50
The Voices Found Under the 43rd St. Viaduct, Brooklyn _ 51
Countermark _ 53
The Widower _ 54
Jackie Bremlin Reflects on his Vaudeville Years _ 55
Broderick Looks up from His Ledger _ 56
New York Getaway _ 57
The Romance of Men _ 58
Janet Three Years Before Her Illness _ 59
Sales Convention _ 60
The Girl in Blue _ 61
Little Johnny Daydreams About the Day Trip to the Stockyards _ 62
The Spirit of Remembrance _ 63
Karen, Coming of Age in Ottawa, Ohio _ 64
The Angel Fish are Fifty Cents Each _ 65
Rain and the Afternoon _ 66
Charlie Remembers that He Has Been Here Most of his Life _ 67
Monique Arrives in New York _ 68
Mona; the Flower of Greenwich Village _ 69
The Parson Walks Out into his Backyard Under the Moon _ 70
The Remember Widowing _ 71
The Man With No Heart _ 72
Almanac _ 74
1956, A Year of Promise _ 75
The New Start _ 76
Sally Wonders in New Haven _ 77
What is Perfect About the American Woman _ 78

These Princesses _ 79
Forget-me-nots _ 80
The Dashing Newsmen of Paris March on a Blue Cloud _ 83
Jeremy on His Fourth Summer Cruise _ 85
Fanny of Omaha Wins a Trip _ 86
The Year of Promise _ 87
What is Tough for Children _ 88
At Home _ 89
Proposal _ 90
Things I Still Want _ 91
Vista Dome _ 93
Some Birds Go Southwest _ 94
Desert Voice _ 95
California Zephyr _ 97
I Promise You This _ 98
Taking an Afternoon Drive on the Coast _ 99
Moving to California _ 100

Hooray for Hollywood _ 101
I Worship You _ 103
Bobby Kitonin Clears his Throat _ 104
Springtime in Hollywood _ 105
The Jet Revolution _ 106
The First American Man Flies Over History _ 107
The Man Who Played Cochise _ 108
Tempo 57, Or the Man Who Watched Too Much TV _ 109
Hollywood Hairdresser _ 110
The Notion of Envy at Paramount's Canadian News _ 111
Jack Parr _ 112
The Sometimes Date _ 113
Shelley Winters _ 114
I Am the Cheery Melody of 1955 _ 115
What's in it for Miss America? _ 116
Her Agent _ 117
Give This Note to the Woman Alone _ 118
The Tonight Show _ 119
Talking to His Manager _ 120

The Art Critic Dashes his Brains Against a Rock in Arches National
    Park, Utah _ 121
Sparky, the TV Dog _ 122
Bob and Ray, TV Comics and Back Taxes _ 123
Liberace _ 124
After Losing His Wife To Insanity _ 125
Waking Thoughts of the Stars _ 126
The Moon and Frank Sinatra _ 131
His Memory _ 132
Jack Parr Leaves the Network _ 134
Shangrila _ 135
A Little Fat Man Rises from a Leather Chair _ 136

Sweeney at the Chesapeake Lounge

How to Receive Signals

Suppose you are listening to a dramatic show, for example,
suppose you are listening to the fifties.
Suppose the console is everywhere. Suppose you
can hook up the microphone to raindrops in Peoria.
Suppose the volume of each voice is so raised as to make
a soundtrack for what you have shut out—the live
musicians of your life; what was absorbed and forgotten.
Suppose there are many programs recorded simultaneously,
and are sometimes interrupted, and the sender consists of
heartbreak, just like you, of joy and love, the electrical image
of what mixes and balances in your harmonies. The voices, the music,
the carrier waves of grief, in buildings, on seashores; suppose you
have a distant message—buzzers, chimes, from bells to gravel paths
and moonlight dinners. Suppose these can be stored in the library of
your mind and you can hear sooner or later the sound of an orchestra
that uses a special broadcast, telling the actors what to do, while
the program is on the air.
Suppose the distance of icebergs and buses and trains and
the shorelines, and babies and passenger ships and planes.

Pick up the passengers. Buy their signature. Identify someone.
Inform yourself.
What is it to be without a radio?
It is to be in the homes of the many in the 1950's,
in a special two-way broadcast, tracking the paths of the
rockets in a condition of space.

What an Adult Would Watch

Taking a tour of Baltimore County
by way of 1946.
The soul of me and what an adult would watch.

The widely celebrated Kidoodlers
are appearing at the Biltmore Lounge.

Look at the widely celebrated Kidoodlers,
widely dead,
grinning, smiling, seething
at the NBC microphone.
Here is the sentiment, come to visit,
the visiting sentiments
at the Hotel Stafford,
Mt. Vernon Place,
Maryland cooking at its best.
The Hutzler Fountain Shop where
old friends meet.
Mother Mueller's Restaurant and Lounge.
Hi-Ho Inn.
Beer, wine, liquors.
Kick off with cocktails and luncheon at
Eddie Leonard's Spa and Bar.

Peace is wonderful.
Hollywood makes amends.

There's the Lyric Theater,
and by special arrangement
Tamara Toumanova, the world famous ballerina,
supported by the Baltimore Symphony Orchestra,
for matinee and evening performances,
for the Armistice Day Matinee.

Then there is the rollicking new sailor ballet,
Fancy Free, a story in dance of three sailors
on shore leave in search of companionable
feminine partners. This is featured in the afternoon

and evening programs.
Keep in mind a galaxy of stars.
Keep in mind the local footlights.
Keep in mind the song birds and the basso buffos,
and the great singing comedians.
and Rosa Ponselle and the Chilean baritone,
both from the Met.

Keep in mind today is stage
and tomorrow is tragedy,

and *Blossom Time*.
Keep in mind the much-loved *Blossom Time*
at the Ford Theatre,
and the music and the musical biography
behind flowers in Carroll County
and the lovemaking
and regular matinees.

Keep in mind we are virtually all strolling
into the comprehensive ideas of when we
were kids,
and dancing and there are open hydrants and
telephone poles,
and shacks and the Ambassador Theatre,
and the moon on the inside and the walk
to the Peabody Conservatory, and the Edgar
Allan Poe statue and Washington Square.

Keep in mind the town
and the calendar of worthwhile events,
the events of the heart for the week beginning
Saturday, November 11th and ending
with the rest of your life.

Keep in mind wrestling and racing and dancing
and stages and concerts.
Keep in mind that you are a child of thirteen,

watching the smile of the world in your smile,
remembering the fall season as if it were
in you, the world in you,
and outside, and

you are its presentation.

Sweeney

I'd like to talk of Sweeney at the Chesapeake Lounge, he is
so happy steppin' out of the Hotel Emerson, with an
indefinable quality about him, and a spacey air. He is a
theatre-goer, he is money on the rag, he is a jockey that is
naturally gratified, never never cashes a ticket without a tête-à-tête.
He is happy with cocktails at the Robert Myer Hotel. He is happy with
horn on horns at the Chicken Roost. Sweeney I love you, you have
Baltimore in spades, and a sixth war loan. Sweeney, where are ya?
Dancin' at the Alcazar, at the Cathedral at Madison? Here, I see you at
the burlesque backstage, see you at the 2 O'Clock Club,
or is it the Chungking at 2 a.m.?
Sweeney, do you go where old friends meet?
Sweeney, are you still with Estelle Slavin?
I send you a monumental memo.
I want a brief talk, I wanna continue walkin' with you,
past summer, past the rehabilitation programs,
past all the dinners served at the Parkway.

The controversy is still raging.
I am with you. Click with those birds of time,
Maria Montez comin' to visit. Sweeney, I am your
public diary. The stalwarts of time have faded into
previous seasons, where we were fledglings, important enough
to fill the universe, the continuous record of heartbreaks.

I am your comic, Sweeney.
Every evening, the moon takes over Taos.
The date falls, today or any other day.

You are time on an evening bill.

A Picture Book of Baltimore

Colonial lattices with their own birch trees.

Representatives like Roman Legions at
the 1912 Democratic National Convention,

an engraving of mayhem during rioting.

A charming couple of 1860;
his legs crossed, so poised he looks suspended.
A black upside down buttercup for a gown.

Judges dressed like black marauders before
a boulder sized globe of the world.

The Hopkins Banjo Club,
a group of seals with banjos.

An athletic team dressed like French
prisoners.

✯

The cruise ship Argentina,
like a starched collar.

Trucks like pups under gantries.

An aerial view that looks like a
floral arrangement but is actually
60 thousand people at the Navy–Notre Dame football
game.

Rooftops with fireflies that is actually
the view looking west from Broadway
at night.

Rosa Ponselle coming down the Opera House
stairs like the Winged Victory.

The Harlem Park dwelling units,
stacked crates.

A drawing of the new main post-office
with cars mirrored by the same-sized clouds.

Remember

Because we love these people, at the
exact state of our lifetime, because we love
these people we have a sentiment that embraces famous
cowboys and the Valencia Club, because of time, we love,
because of time, the killer, because of time, the fine
musician that clicks solidly past us, teams up nicely, with
Alice and Fay and little Georgia, who handles herself mercifully—
time, because the current cinema is my heart, time that walks
into a mid-town apartment and proclaims the purely personal.

I am at the Club Charles, on Wednesday and Thursday,
with a smile.
I give you all the dinner rhythms, I give you all the
carnations and the music you want.
I give you the twilight tunes.
I give you the *Invitation Waltz,* and
the familiar music of your grandparents,
the concert miniatures of your heart.

Keep your ear attuned, go for a bite at the China Inn,
go to the Madison and don't pass without saying hello

to Cyril Mansfield and his Society Orchestra.
Figure out the last time you were here,
looking in and tipping your hat to the
slight innovation of that lovely bandaged heart;
figure out the least way to be naturally gratified;
wrap the picture up some years ago.

Sit with an indefinable quality.

See your celebration—
death with the dignity of a flicker house.

The Purely Personal

Baltimore, my Baltimore
I am your public diary.
Don't look with disfavour on me,
there is one strange thing, my heart
behind the eight ball,
and many disadvantages in my memory.
There are people that insisted "yes";
there are people that didn't seem to mind
the slums. Look in my heart,
see the entertainers, see the
broken down streets, see the reasons
for my advancing grief; do not look
with disfavour. Do not look at
every evening grave.

Is Baltimore a hick town? I shall say *no*. Memory will make
amends. It is in the nature of streets,
and in the nature of familiar contempt.
It is in the nature of a keen sense of pleasure.
But the strange thing is that I insist
that Baltimore, despite the
disadvantages of my memory,
moves with a love of graves and gatherings.

Pimlico

Pimlico adds to my life.
Blossom Time. Look what returns to
Baltimore, The Ford Theatre, after a successful
engagement: Ruth Gilette, in *Blossom Time,* an
atmosphere of a tender and loving story. *Blossom Time*
gives us lovers of music, *Blossom Time* with its happy
matinees. This is the 1947 revival of *Blossom Time,*
with a lovely score and original melodies.

The cast is virtually in sunlight.

Sweeney at the Chesapeake Lounge

Here we have a new singing sensation.
The trumpets are blaring for us.
Do we look puzzled?
No, we're having a good time
at the Chanticleer, at the White Rice Inn,
at Marty's;
"Carlo's and Cheetah," the musical comedy
dance; "Leona," the cover girl chanteuse—
the Gayety and the Ralph Diaz Unit,
the Club 21, the Girlesque show at the
Two O'Clock Club.

I am Sweeney at the Chesapeake Lounge;
I am the purely personal come to visit.
I am the Melody Boys, the Arundel Blue Room,
I am Baltimore in the fifties on Friday,
around town without a script.

I turn around slowly into the Pimlico Park Drive
and I'm
dreaming the nite-life.

Seduction Song

Sweeney says c'mon and dance
(I advise you to keep your eye on your girl)
log the music with me, wax philosophical with
those eyes; no prima donna passages, look like
a card dealer who is in love, loveable and likeable,
come dance with me! We need no match to get this
fire goin'. You can play this under an assumed name.
We are Roseland history.
Forget one reason or another. You are
my simple arithmetic. I love you tonight like
music out of the North, you are my sweet, carried
further than the swallows of the bay.
I'm a big fish in a little pond, my Sally. Look risky, for
time is a listener reaction waitin' for autumn.
Time is where the street's goin' and we'll get there
ahead. Just dance!
There's Mable Mercer and her new flame. There's
Katie, the purveyor of genial men, and sweetness and
light puttin' the last couple of years out of business,
puttin' the illness away, makin' a solo horn out
of grief. Come dance with me! Forget society.
Forget the war and the old-timers.
There's medleyin' into the streets with me!
It's almost a cinch to do it well,
easy as music, a one nighter,
and a bright and fancy smile.

Shore Leave

Baltimore, 1948, and Sally Rose
delighting the Madison fans; there's more and more and fine food
in the Bar and Cocktail lounge and the Armed Forces
on furlough. There is the Girlesque Show. There is the
Arundel Blue Room and a few miles away Karl Krueger conducts
the Detroit Symphony, *The Master Race* showing at the
Hippodrome Theatre, Warner Brother's Stanley is showing
The Very Thought of You, Dennis Morgan, Eleanor Parker ...
we could go every week. This is wonderful, Baltimore, my
Baltimore, talk about the Navy–Cornell game and Ford's Theatre,
and the Playshop bill and the *Dial-Twisters;* oh the pity of
it all, to page a hero, a hero after the war, to go to
Howard's, near Center Street and watch *The Very Thought of You.*
Isn't it grand to dine and dance where we want, at the
Madison Club, at the Piccadilly?

I am the purely personal come to visit.
In the G.I. radio programs—the Armed Forces and the
men of the services saluted every Tuesday and
Thursday; I stand by the Hutzler's downstairs
store, and wait for Lois de Fee, the head dancer.
Lois de Fee, where are you? Long slim legs. Did you
dance at the Alcazar?
Where is that fur you were wearing?
Where are the strange animals and birds and insects?

Lois de Fee is the tallest girl in burlesque.
Watch her comedy twins, at the Turf-Bar and
Cocktail Lounge.
Watch the Girlesque Show.
Watch the China Clipper.
Watch and dine and dance at Murray's.
Let's get around to the Hotel Emerson.

Maggie on the Dotted Line

Nite life; find the big band, find Joe Castro, Serge Chelov,
and Eddie Shu; there's a high hat startin' with a wood sheddin' beat;
Tony Bennett at the Latin Quarter.
Are you temporarily without a date? Try pianos
and tin angels, and Big Jay McNealy at the Capital.
Quite wonderful! Quite wonderful! Maybe you'll
meet and marry; maybe with big champagne at Mahogany Hall
you'll find a happy beau! Try the " blue note" try the "high note"
for God's sake find your happiness.
Take a glance at the boys in the reed section, and the brass too.
Dance all over the floor. Shine!
Find your leading role, your own, with a
late arrival and a crazy rhythm, as
moonlight floats you
over the casino gardens.

Nite-Life

At the Gayety there's a real honest-to-goodness show, flowin'
with talent; Friday. It is billed as a star-studded special, with
Billy Scratch as the headliner, and the Picadilly Pipers and the
Four Ginger Snaps at Eddie Leonard's Spa and Musical bar.
Phil Brito is in the Algerian Room; the Biltmore Lounge features
Eileen and the Delta Rhythm Boys.
Milton Lyon's music at the Aragon Tavern,
and Baltimore's slumming spot, the Club Picadilly, features
burlesque shows and a chorus of beautiful girls.

I wanna be at the Chesapeake Lounge.
I wanna be at the Chesapeake lounge and kick-off with
cocktails and luncheon, and touch down with dinner and dancing,
with Cyril Mansfield and his orchestra, his Society Orchestra.

I wanna go to Sweeney's for a sultan's night of poker.
I wanna stop off at Murray's Chicken-Roost restaurant
in East Baltimore,
for it is never closed.

Meeting the Challenge of a Changing world

There is the skyline of Baltimore,
the Sun Square on V-E day,
the smiles on the young faces.
An impressive post-war visitor,
I stand at Fort McHenry,
and shout to Sweeney, who didn't fight
in Europe, cuz he was mostly a local breed,
but he's a lion in his own right, defyin' Max
Hochschild and Jimmy Hutzler. He may even
have been at the opening ceremonies of
Eastpoint Shopping Center in 1956.
Sweeney too was a battle for survival and rebirth,
like all of us, a bird's-eye view of relief that the
sun has come up another day.

He walks by the fighter planes at the Martin plant
like a son who has returned. He walks down
Howard Street with a detachment of gobs.
He stops by the barber shop,
and waves to Sidney, his Pimlico pal and
grins at Johnson, cuz they'll meet at Madison and Chester
to pick up Sally Stapleton, the pleasant dispensation of
Fayette.
There is pettishness in the crisp afternoon air of Essex.
It is before Elvis and Orbison, and everyone is thinkin'
they know a communist. There are distorted facts,
but men of high character, cut like Sweeney say
"shush," I'll show you around town and omit the childish.
He has a date with Giordano at the Mecca.
They'll play poker 'til the night takes up the slack.
He takes the Eastern Avenue bus to City Hospital,

and drops in on his Broadway pal, Joe Pratt, in memory of
the oyster fleets they put away in summers past.

Sweeney Would Have Liked Route 66

Sweeney would have liked Route 66,
not that he'd ever get to somethin' so hot and
sandy, and pulling out of Needles to get to California.
Sweeney is single and sassy, and doesn't wear
tight t-shirts, although he would have liked the
sausage farm and pastries along the road.
Sweeney is a combination man, and a verve to boot.
Sweeney likes music in review, and he calls it
the night sky. I think he might even have a thing for
Lee Wiley singin' *West of the Moon*. He's not too
tied up to any school of thought. He is a
jazz man extraordinaire. No chocolate croissants
and witty arrangements of talk. He is the beauty and
the beast, and the beauty is himself, pushin' it as
a single guy, happy to dream of The Lazy Nugget Ranch in Vegas;
and when he thinks of Cleopatra and other stories
he is thinkin' Maxine as a tragedy in white at the burlesque.
Whoosh! There goes a Buick special convertible.
      On rare nights he walks his demon round the town,
and shops for a second chance at youth.

Smiley Burnette

Cowboy comedian Smiley Burnette is appearing on the
Hippodrome stage, and at the Parkway; the yarn concerns all of us.
There's Eleanor Parker at the Pasadena, James Mason at
the Paramount; at the Valencia, they are showing
Abroad with Two Yanks, at the Mount Royal Hotel, Bill Stoos,
Mary Lotree, her accordion songs; at Keefs, Lexington near Parks,
there's somethin' embellished in Technicolor, and the Demon's Club
presents the Mammoth Magic Show. Oh world. Oh time.
Marriage is a Private Affair at the Parkway.
Maisie Goes to Reno at the Century,
and Smiley Burnette on stage in person; my pal, the wolf of time
is here. That maniacal physician, with a good voice and tears,
and the lover of young girls who will grow old. At the Gayety,
a gala show, Maxine DeShon, a daring newcomer.
The natural situations of life are coming to visit,
with affection, under that kindly housekeeper, the sun.
These are weaving stories, and the synthetic, dramatic treatments,
the sustained entertainment of time, with troublesome antics.

The cathedral at Madison Avenue bows down.
Five soldiers walk by, on furlough.

My pal, the wolf of time, the sleeper among the entries,
a smart murder mystery called nostalgia.

The famous cowboy comedian, Smiley Burnette, has a
Svengali formula. He smiles.
So that time becomes a young singer
that gives you affection and loyalty,
and a light characterization of love.

Burlesque Queen

Ann Corio sees the light.
She's finally seen the light.

I think I'll keep trackin' the stars.

Enoch, who is more beguiling?
Who is the fairest strip-teaser
of them all?
Who is taking things in stride?

Music does something to me, Mister, says Ann Corio.
Don't talk to me about commercialism, don't talk
about the fiddle,

don't talk about recovering the ground on which
we've lost our time.
Don't you think I should keep my clothes on for a change?

I'm going to nix out of this glorious summer.
I'm going to nix out, and keep my clothes on for a change.

The Music Scene, 1947

Charlie Spivak's got a beautiful horn
and a fog of rumour surrounds him.
Charlie Spivak's got no questions.
He's goin' overboard on finding himself a
style
and won't play exhibition horn.

Buddy Yeager's go horn works, for the books,
and Mrs. Berlin gets a tie-up with the USO;
everyone's angle is wine and dining and
dancing, and
the plugging of discs.

Los Angeles and the separation of NBC and
the blue network...

Hazel Scott whose busty pianoings have been
starred in café society....

Everybody is beautiful here.
The Red Sox and the Tigers are dancing.
A newshound snaps a picture of the
T. Dorsey band.
Sinatra looks like a riff-raff jitterbug.

Everybody is beating their brains out about
tires and gas...

yip yap, yip yap.

(New York publicity has turned the
secretary's desk around.)

Of Sweeney

That's warm—that's Harry Belafonte...
that's sentimental—that's Eddie Fisher...
that's smooth...that's Frank Sinatra.
No time for the blues.

There's gentle...the star of NBC's hour long Perry Como show.
There's mellow...the popular Nat King Cole.
That's sensitive...that's Johnny Ray.
Inventive? Little Sammy, who looks forward to everything.

You want tender? Go for Bill Hayes.
You want energetic? Go for Frankie Lane.
You want endearing?
    Try Sweeney at the Chesapeake Lounge.
    I vote for the one I like best. Sweeney in the playin' field.
    My lone flight vocalist, pictured in 1948, on a little honeymoon
    with life.
Cuz, he avoids thinkin' about the problems of the day for
the first half hour after he gets up.
Cuz he loves meteorites, cuz they remind him of
his school days.
He loves the dark, because the path of the moon
round the earth is not a true one, cuz he's
never too hard on Santa, in the true Christmas spirit.

He sends flowers, and wants to meet Arlene Austin,
the junior Miss Society editor of the Bell-Flower Herald-American.

Good ol' Sweeney, with a life that calls for a mature woman,
who books extras, and doesn't quite recall what he did on his
second date.

And So We Sing the Musics

And so we sing the musics that Sweeney loves;
The Dundalk strike threat is over,
Jess junks the band and Billy Ducats likes hot cakes.
Rory, mov'er over! Chubby blasts, and
Charlie Ventura leaps to town. The 408 Bar opens
and music and plot come closely and closer to
Sweeney's night song.
He is tied in with the breeze at midnight.
It bears his name, and he looks like it. He
jumps in earnest, a local cat, and in the early morning,
with the spots shut down, he sings slow tunes and fine ballads in
his mind, a night clubber for the sweet ballrooms.
Just me, just me. *How High the Moon*, he whispers into
his hat. In the interlude between dawn and sunset,
he is the spite in everybody's melody, but
the joy
in melancholy prediction.
November opens with cold, but he is fit and versatile,
knockin' down the chatter and the tight watch of the years.
He's got no gilded version of what life does.
He is a Mardi Gras in a wired brain.
At a local Sunday bash, he shows up a little brighter
for a band that clicks his way.

Voices Wafting Through the Severna Park Marina

The Tip Top girls, direct from Hollywood
and recent screen successes, and the magical gesture
and master of ceremonies in the Moon-Glo Club
of the Severna Park Marina.
Twelve lovely ladies in perpetual motion in a dazzling
array of dress and undress. *Night of the Shanghai* and
introducing *Fiddlin' for the Czar*, a revelation
in entertainment. Twelve lovely ladies and dancers from
the Argentine who do American swing. All for a dollar fifty.

Tonight is yours. Beautiful girls will dance for you,
golden voices will sing for you.
Everything you may want shall be yours, merely to command.
The orchestra leader is your servant of melody;
the waiter, your servant of food. The tender of the bar—
at your service.

Tonight you are a king.
Tonight you are a queen.

A Date with Sweeney

There is everythin', Sweeney says.
Nothin' to be scared about. Just droppin' in on
Rudy Vasco and his Latin American quartet,
lookin' up to date and spiffy, struttin' his barbecue,
wonderin' 'bout Maxine DeShon, the year's "thrill girl" at
the Gayety.
      He pokes the bell at the front door, takes pains
to polish his shoes. He is one of God's men, the daydreamer.
The noise of women's voices makes him think of
New York, which was his home, makes him
fierce like a Chinese boy with lots of advice.
      Isn't she marvelous?
         The final decision shows up at the door.
"Never mind ol' girl" and with a loud cry flings his
arms around her.
      It is 1947. Long legged and rangy,
        he drops a shoe and buys a bag of popcorn and emits a
          comical groan.

      Peeping through midnight noises,
they cry together, and tell each other secrets.

Pining

The hungry awful men of 1949 are screaming
Save us, save us from the ballrooms and the tears,
and the Burns Quartet. It may be love we're after,
it may be love. It may be heaven. It may be we
line up at the office. Maybe we line up at the
office to see Ann Corio, to see the light, to see Charlie Barnet and
his crew on the edge.
It may be we just want to be away.
It means we want to be away. It may be love.

It may be the hit parade we're after, and a song-pickin' method.
But we doubt it.

We are the blue notes,
we are the blue notes,
dickering for Edison.

Dirge for Sidney

Sidney got it in an alley,
callin' for someone's attention,
a knife in the gut,
the leisurely approach of two strangers,
maybe behind the Blue Mirror, while
Cora Walsh and her accordion songs romanced
the premises; my pal the wolf of time snuck up
on Sidney, known for nothing but
his spectacles and a fish handshake, a so and so
barber slapped with pranks, who lived with his mother,
disappearin' in the nite life; there was the other side of
fun after dark. Giordano who took the
health funds to Vegas, and Billy Kane who made hell for
his daughter at Mortar Creek.
Sidney, with cobwebs in his wallet, steppin' to his
favourite flicker house, a notable addition to
Baltimore's slim list of murders. Lighted well enough,
are you lighted well enough, Sidney, to return to the
Biltmore, for the legendary, for the
convalescin' from life?
Sidney had a face that can be charitably described
as somethin' attuned to a wish.
Strangers found him, for the cobwebs in his wallet,
and the stars resumed with a vengeance
over the Baltimore Stadium, over the Locust Point Ferry.

Johnson

Johnson got it too. Stabbed in a fight.
But Johnson would have high-kicked back,
unhappy to soil his own shoes.
Johnson was the shoe-shine man at the
barber shop, trim-jacketed and a winning smile,
lean as a tap-dancer, and heard to be a ladies' man.
The shiniest shoes in the world. Mirrors;
Johnson's hand could whip along your toes—
the self-same hands that
wiggled the beauties on Lombard Street; the ecstasies
those hands could give, and a lustre to your shoes,
and a winning smile.
He lived for ladies. Spiffy, white teeth.
He was a doo-wop group, compressed.
He had the smile of Jesus, self-assured,
and circumspect with words. He knew just
what to say, and precious little.
He did a job so menial as to perfect his art,
a dandelion on the planet.

The Men of Jazz

They've got somethin' to say;
the mayor's men in the alley, the swingers of the Bay Bridge—
the ragtime marches on;
the mole recalls Capone,
and there's Skitch Henderson and his
Atlantic tour; here comes the
band via Pennsylvania's Café Rouge,
with no fear of pleasin'.
They speak for themselves.

The Harmony Mutes,
the Roxies at Regalia, the Moonies;
saxophonist Caesar, the masters jivin' the
blackouts and the antics.

They are the Martinique of a few years ago,
the nice things, and the goodly music, the jazz,
the migration of stars,
the died-out broadcasts,
the waxing discs,
harmonicas and whistlers, and
ripplin' rhythms.

We have a grave problem.
The utterance that influenced the nation amounts to
age versus youth—Jolson versus 1947;
what is postponed is entirely out of whack
with *My Blue Heaven*.

The migration is commencin',
with round be-boppers and a heat wave
plottin' out the time;
and time is the issue that hits the streets,

with its own idioms.

Bongo Intro

Some tunes depart from limbo, tenderly in the
moonlight, *Tin Roof Blues, Redhead Gal*. That's my opinion,
but limbo is not good enough, what with the
emotion and rhythm, what deserves special mention, a trance,
and an immediate intonation.

Home Again Blues, Haggar's Blues, Love Nest, to fall
into the abyss of forgetfulness the first time I heard
All One Winter sung by the tenor sax player. I don't despair;
Sweetheart and *Home Again, Honeysuckle Rose*. What deserves
special mention— limbo is not good enough. Limbo is not
good enough. It is time to express my
very own sentiments,
to say revivals are jazz beauties,
in the abyss of forgetfulness.
Let's return to America later,
and right after it, with one vote less.
Let us create a splendour
of emotion and rhythm.
Also,
rosy cheeks and bright eyes,
and *Hard-hearted Hanna*.

What is dear to my heart?
Ideal tunes for a season.
B.J. Halliday.

I went on the three hour trip to Philadelphia.
To talk to Lionel Hampton. Nobody knew
None of my Jelly-Roll.

Sphinx.
Sudan.
Right after them.

The Jive Pigs

Songs to sing, oh, blow out the storm! It's Dizzy, the pig;
I just slide down the banister one more time, lift the cover and
the followin' day find myself engaged to an impertinence.
Well give me some pigskin, that might be the case.
Here comes the wolf!
What's a square deal? One day three little pigs were
relaxin' on the porch—oopopadow! There's three
little pigs. Can you reach them? You know that the
approach was the business of constructing suitable shelter.
Top o' the big bash! Here's the clinker ... the wolf leaps out in
E-flat, Man! Fall in. And the wolf falls in,
down the chimney, into his favourite soup:
cream of nowhere.

The Future from Grant Street

Now you know what brings me here.

Soon the beatniks will spin into eclipse,
yet it's still an art.
Grant mounts the Everest of Upper Bohemia,
and language can find itself.

And today the bearded baffled beatniks and pastel shades,
and their brief latin moods, are changed as chameleons.

Chinatown ends abruptly at Broadway
and beyond this neighborhood, no one will be satisfied.

The stars drop sharply to the Embarcadero docks.
A gull watches impassively,
from the casements of art.

Elegy for a Drummer
or "asking a swing ghost about the secrets of time."
for B.J. Halliday

B.J. here we go; you weren't famous as a drummer, but
you were stricken, crippled from the joy of the world
perhaps, lookin' for a jump session, *Rainbow over Paradise,*
Sweet Cona Noonlight, My Hop Hula Hula Girl; these are
your favourites you lonely jive fan you. You and the
blue eyes, clink clink and a drink, bright and two step.
What do you know about my youth crippled in
the life of Baltimore? *Animal March, Honolulu Sweetheart of Mine;*
you are my art, B.J.; you are my hunchback, you are my fall
that made perhaps the welding complete. *The Sheik of Araby*
and *Those Swingin' Doors, Waltz, I'll Get By,* voca-dance, voca-dance,
jump the fences, jump at a julep joint. Find a companion
find a nice quiet girl.

I wish you rest, Halliday.

Katie and John

When Katie and John danced
    —of course they did nothing but dance—
brought up kids, but were out dancing every
chance they got, dance partners
who widowed everybody—
the polka, the fox trot. Dance partners
at 80. Cheap as hell, mouthy as
the devil. Put it aside.
They danced.

John broke his leg in the old folks home
and died of complications.
Katie, demented, waiting for John,
wanting to dance, and John has one leg and waits
somewhere. You might say
they were born to dance.
They were good at nothing else.
And sanctified each other,
in that way, in Maryland.

Sweeney's Ghost Speaks to me

I'm not surprised at the fidelity of this city,
I'm not surprised at this point under the forthcomin'
stars, one hundred and seven of them, resultin'
in unseasonably cold weather, that's my heart—
unseasonably cold weather, chastisin' itself
in Baltimore, from winter to April, the passing march
of time, with no breaks. I wear the season well.
I wield a firm gavel and bring it down, restored
to the air once more.
Baltimore. The name lingers like memory,
like questions of love,
at my own request.
The contract reads, questions of love.
It is my inspiration to need you in
such musics as circle my heart.

Round Again Record

Baltimore,
deep with no solution,
the middle ages of my world,
where every character has a talent,
where every musician has a
solution hit, where dreams and some
desires are found under the boardwalk,
some checkin' up on Federation Street, some
checkin' on train-thumpin', shell-jinglin', pipe-
blowin'. No problems emerge out of this
Baltimore, except the emergence of
love. Who pays? How much?
A justifiable pride, I walk toward you my Maryland,
if not with an esoteric group of music fanciers, then
by myself, alone, a small boy, with
difficulty, trying to free
the voices of his heart; free
of the delusion that music is sent directly
from heaven. Where, with his talent unmolested,
under the music makin' stars, the roar of
sea-waves pounds against him, tom-tom thumpin'
like a bird on a bough,
he whispers, "Am I home"?

CAVALCADE

Weather and the Fifties

Plotters and station models
wind speeds and directions;
what is a mass of warm air overtaking, the
rainstorm approaching, and continued fair weather?
These are weather facts, and there are idea facts,
the migrations of birds, and continued rain or snow
and sadness, and falling temperatures, careful observations
of the heart. There are temperature patterns and moisture,
the character of grief indicated. What makes up the weather?
Tears, heartbreak, joy, exhilaration, weather vanes,
air pressure, and the effect of love.

Are there attempts to control the weather, are there
flags and lights and storm warnings, for a sea of love?
There are calm regions and horse latitudes and tropospheres,
and sunspots and the rain on Mrs. Haggerty's porch and the
chirping cricket, and the foggiest places in the world, and the
driest places in spring and autumn, there are the differences
between love and death, and alto-cumulous clouds
gathering in Chicago, and jet-streams that bring music,
and equators that sink into the remembered.

There are weather patterns we do not clearly understand.
Shine a flashlight on them. Guide a beam straight down onto
a piece of paper. The light will recover for you the love,
the want, the absorption of colour,
the dreams of the dead.

The Red-Headed Widow

There is no chance for a red-headed widow,
not here, not anywhere.
Why?

He was half-way in love with me.
Why?
It was after the funeral.

And the sun began to set after a big bank of
clouds,
and that's the way it's been for weeks.

My heart caught fire, my heart caught
fire, because I thought he was a man.
He came to see me, angry as a lion,
and I waited by the mesquite and the
chaparral,
and the little brown prairie sang to me,
and I wept into the barn,
I wept by lantern-light,
I wept by the emptiness.
I went to the house and remembered the
invalid of past years.

There is a strange longing in my fingers.

The war goes on, and it is not dark, yet.

I watch them go.
I always watch them go.

The Bow of the Missouri and Frank Marsden, Looking at the Waves the Night Before

The battleship has many things.
It has energy, it has flames.
There are Korean rocks.
There are lights flashing in the pitch of night,
and America,
made up of her children,
and giant guns.

That's what it is to die,
that's what it is to leave home inside.

This is different,
and someday,
the modern battleship will be
America's strength,

and I am the first line

in an ever growing spring.

On the North Atlantic

There is a beautiful
discipline rewarded.
It converts both man and woman.

There is the inherent in
men of all ages,

and the sheer deep-rooted faith.

There are qualified divers and parts of history.
There are anti-aircraft batteries.
There are days that go in and out,

and all these things and more,
go out to sea.

The Armistice Day Matinee

Welcome to the Armistice Day Matinee.
It is a rollicking sailor ballet,
fancy free. It is the
Armistice Day Matinee,
with the *Queen of the Swans,*
and Paul Petroff's *Prince Siegfried,*
the story and dance of three
sailors on the shore,
in search of companionable women.
In the afternoon and evening,
the Armistice Day Matinee, and the
singing comedians,
the dead.

Back from Bellevue Psychiatric Hospital, 1951

Why did we ever live in a G.I.
town? With the veteran and his wife.
How did we live when the war ended,

when our name finally came up,
on the college trailer list. How are the four
walls and the barracks apartment? Why was I almost
alone for three years?
Why have I wondered, with all my experience?

Why have I determined that the war never ended?

How should I return?
How should I find union?
There is a letter every five hours.

There is a far away husband.
There is the trivia of college.
There is a medal and a time
for seldom-worn jackets.

I am touched.
I am a facsimile.
I am in the home of a widow.

I want to be her quiet kerosene lamp.

Spinster Set

She liked the soldiers, of course
she did; she laughed, she laughed, she cried,
she danced with them. Perhaps she was too
careful by the canteen?

What does it matter?
With Colin she knew she could never be
alone again. Instinctively she turns to him,
instinctively, as if she had known him
a long, long time. She is so glad.
She parts bravely, and her heart is beating
with a little sound.

She meets him one day, after the
stars have closed their lattices,
and he feels it too.

He feels the generosity of wind.
He laughs and pulls her hand to his;
they are fearful and on guard.
And new. And ecstatic,
and yearn
with one voice.

We Ran Together in the Rain.

Are we happy? There's nothing
world shaking here, we are suddenly young
again, in love in the first time of our life.
Are we happy here?
Are we suddenly in the world again, are we
in love? May we run together in the rain, always.
What is world shaking about this?
It shakes my world,
for suddenly, I am young again,
and in love.

What is the Nature of the Dead Men of the Fifties?

An empty vacation spot for the whole family.
A life unsupervised.
Square dancing and nature study excursions.

Everyone working for happiness.
To find a state that glows,
and wonderful weeks,
and seamen regaining consciousness.
Hundreds of times in the darkness and light,
witnessing the miracle of rain, to
inhale a breath with intonations and mannerisms,

to go to Long Island and find a strange enchanted alchemy,
and each leaf in the shape of a floating glory.

To be beyond the dark days of war.
To love trailer life.
To think of professors as men too mature to
follow empty dogma.

The big question.
That nature is a face and a story, a kind of
experience in which one recognizes a boy's
unusual talent, a girl soon noticing the lighted
face of her years.

The nature of the dead men of the fifties,
is to have sympathy enter the heart through
the eyes, like providence.

And to see the hand of humanity in
the sharecroppers, and in Dallas, the beautiful.

Is in leaving Dixie to drive north.
To peel the feelings away, and to find one's possessions
in a short biography of love.

Barfly, Jack Arema

I don't know how the
best man can ever win in a world like this.

If I hadn't happened to park my car,
if I hadn't gone inside,
if Mulvany had been less than a half-century old;
Mulvany had waitresses!

He had all the girls he wanted.
I'll have a cup of coffee and wait with
a cool, low-pitched, male voice.

I turn and stuff the handkerchief back
in my jacket; I turn around and
ask "what is your name"?

She gives me a puzzled look.
She seems anxious,
she serves me a salad instead of water.

I resign myself to letting things happen.
I resign myself to being anxious and worried.
I look forward to every night.
I look forward to wall paper in my hotel room.

I am capable.
I hear "yes sir,"
under a gaudy overdose of make-up.

The Voices Found Under the 43rd St. Viaduct, Brooklyn

A kaleidoscope of light and clouds.

An alluring doorway.

Bobby sox girls.

Suede shoes on a sidewalk.
Peep shows and shooting galleries.

Get your picture drawn and your arm tattooed.
Show girls from the canyons west of Broadway.

I bear witness that any woman can be made beautiful.
and I'm caught in the miracle

(and the crowds climb down dark subway stairs).

I am a legend. I belong to no man.

✭

I am weeping because New York is the
biggest ruse there is; the so-called city slickers,
and the city burns with radio skits and
smoking room stories.

There are self-inflated victims
and suckers the size of three bands,
choker necklaces of gorgeous luster,
restaurants and out-of-towners who are shrewd,
price tags and patronizing doctors.
But off the record, I am in a ruse-infested,
paradise, I am suspicious.
I am morose.

New Yorkers think I am a wise guy,
under the 14th Street moon.

★

I have a healthy curiosity about sex.

From other bell boys I learned methods of
seeing who was wedded or not.

Honeymooners generally wear new dresses
and new suits.

A couple checks in with a man
wearing fancy tailor-mades.

What I learn about women puzzles me,
and I am learning about other things;
speech, jewelry, luggage.

Guests with expensive luggage tip more
than those with battered luggage.

The women in their sixties require a pistol
for protection.

The house doctor is a sympathetic soul.
The house doctor has an ailment.

In a big metropolitan hotel,

it takes months to discover what simply

doesn't exist.

Countermark

The body has adjacencies too. It is reminding,
that is not remembered. It is coloration by coloration.

The feeling of the natural.
What is the feeling of the natural?

The fifties.
What are the natural fifties?

There is language that is ghost,
language independent of
voices, through the fog of
time; what outlives the flesh.

Hunger, desire, a dream.

A new portal:

there is a place in time, where things
have stayed; like mist, voices rise,
like dew;
like incantation,
wanting to arrive.

At night, these men, these voices,
like dreams, search.

The Widower

When December marries May,
I ask myself if there is any
chance for happiness,
I ask myself if May and December can merge;
is it a glorious summertime of love?
Is it alright this way?
Will I love you, darling?
Will you close your eyes and
with a soft choked little sound,
put your arms around me?

Vivian and I were dancing,
and she stopped dancing, and her
angry blue eyes grew wide and dark,

and grew into deep pools of pain,
and we faced each other,
and then we looked at the moon.
Someone was shouting.
I felt strangely weak and light-headed.
I drew her to me.

The moon grew enormous and frightened.
Is there any chance of happiness in a
May-December marriage?
Can May and December merge into
a glorious summertime of love?

The world comes into focus,
and then the figures blur again,
and I am dancing with you.

I love you, but there are deep pools
of pain. On a March evening you lay
your hands on me.
I am not an old man yet. It is
a cold December morning,
and the stars are quivering.

Jackie Bremlin Reflects on his Vaudeville Years

—The Stuart Sisters and The Dancing Lovelies,
and the most baffling and amazing act of this
or any age—

oh Eddie Wald and his orchestra,
oh I would love to delight The Liberty fans
in my capacity as an emcee,

I would convey my final lore,
I would use crisp autumn weekends,
and follow the questions with "talk."

I would follow the pattern of recent years
and appear at the Decca Lounge,
and book the celebrated Kidoodlers and
Bill Stoos and The Four Ginger Snaps
who are dead, as are they all, dead;

I will go to the Hutzler Fountain Shop and
think of Maxim, the Russian Cossack Magician,
and muse on the Algerian Room

which is merely my round about way of saying
I got a laugh out of the way God
campaigned on the false premise, my heart.

I who have stopped at the lowest levels.
I who have distorted facts,

I who got a pleasant surprise,
when the stars spotlighted me,

before and after,
with no faith.

Broderick Looks Up from His Ledger
Fourth Floor, Bainsfield Insurance Company

I am dreaming of the Vermont life,
of elm coves and covered bridges.
I want to be in blends of yellow and red
and purple, on one planet. In the Vermont
forest, you can feel the goodness,
the feel of what mushrooms from human kind
and effaces the gills of grief forever,
and aborts the planet of sorrow.
To be a crystallite formation, to be a
hen-of-the woods, to be everything that
you breathe that is good on the planet, the
spores of hundreds of dreams, rising. I want
to assume the shape of balls, and clubs, and cones
and cups and coral,
of shells and umbrellas and rise to heaven
in the second millennium.
I want to tell a story of how, horrified, I escaped
the rule of thumb world, and refused to remember
anything but the joy of the opening day,
the day when stars and old cats formed a ceremony,
running and shouting while the sun dropped behind the
equinox, and I entered the
procession of the unagonized.

New York Getaway

Is this a wonderful week in New York?
We think it is a wonderful week in New York with
pigeons feeding everywhere and hundreds milling around and
the crowds—oh its simpler to get off in mid-Manhattan, but
we keep flying, lit up against the black waters, and the
Hudson, under the arc lights for a midnight sailing; New York,
New York, with elderly chess players, and
tours that are good for you, tours that are good, mind you, rooms
in a smart hotel, Broadway shows, Martha and Bill, meeting their
evening plane at Idlewild.
Let's go to the breathtaking sight because we need
breathtaking sights; we need to find something of
ourselves, we need to find something of what we had.
Don't let your expression change. Stay the same.
Be the eminent detective of my heart. Let us go to
prehistoric school girl days and not notice the child
that broke in you.
Let us go to New York, without face powder, without
mascara, let us go to New York and reach it by family
car or by train, let us plan a holiday, let us get our
feet wet in the world.
Let us find deep cracks between the doors, let us become
apparent to ourselves, and be the
busiest looms in the sky and moods, let us find moods,
and kiss, and dress without protection. Let us find
the excitement that we need,
the sudden chill of terror that comes just from shouting
"I love you,
I have caught you
like myself."

The Romance of Men

What are forgotten mysteries?
Where are they, the forgotten mysteries?
The strange things that held us in a trance,
the new personalities of autumn, the long arms that
issued from the centre of a cloud, the luminous arms,
that were so vast, the long arms of a previous life,
that made rays, that grew dimmer and seemed to sink deeper
into the water. What is my memory that is so forgotten?
All sunlight casts a shadow. And perhaps, I am a theory of love.
I am a theory of love that fell onto a deep trance-like state. I am
the mystery of love and no language. I who could not
distinguish between the movements of her body and the moon.
I, in the realm of the forgotten. I who was fantastic in her arms,
the luminous point of losing myself; this perhaps the strangest
of all instances, unexplainable and forgotten, the tales of
love have come to visit me in this trance-like state, in this
mixture of the two, my love, and memory.

Janet three years before her illness

I am browsing through my World Book Encyclopedia.
I was really enjoying learning.
There are so many wonders.
What is a wonder?
Ask any teacher or librarian.

There is a home somewhere.
It is wonderful.
It's a new wonderland,
and it's fascinating
and it's lovely learning.

At once the whole world seems.
The wonders that await my whole family.
It's like a wonderful party, what awaits us,
what opens up, before me.

I read happily. I was browsing.
Today, where is the next day for school?

I am your child too.
The World Book is in my arms,
look, all at once, the world, the whole world.

Amazing, the short time, to be more, to
look at the fragments for ten days in the world,
an adventure, and lovely;
the whole world seems like a wonderful story,

and I forgot that I was home.
The time is amazing and short.

Sales Convention

This man's world is where the swindle begins;
it is the toboggan of every day sales.
It is dozens and dozens of announcements
requiring articles and limited budgets.
Thus one cannot pick out a fellow who
manufactures a fiddle-de-doo. Only, Jones is
out 21 bucks.
Who is this hog, Mr. Zelik? Who is this hog with
the "special" bread, the one who can't be recognized because
you see him every four hours, the good guy, the good neighbor,
the tailor after money selling fast and stinging suckers.

The way to get rich is never to have a candid comment
about anything,
to just sigh at the mention of Paris and Coney island.

The Girl in Blue

The girl in blue is coming, the girl in
blue,
she walks in a cell of bright white silence,

she says—honeymoon—I made that perfectly plain.
Honeymoon.
Tonight she says goodbye. Tomorrow she enters again
free and carefree, her thin hands on the smooth white
sheets, the royal voice that seems to invade the heart.
She is the girl in blue, at all hours, with the
seagull eyes, my honeymoon, my honeymoon; life is
automatic, people are being born and dying, but far beyond
the wafting of the wind, the strange winding rustling of what
you can't quite hear, I see the girl in blue, in silence,
reaching far down the street, looking for me; strikingly
beautiful, beside the water of the Hudson River,
on a day like any other, in my heart.

Little Johnny Dreams
About the Day Trip to the Stockyards

The stockyard butchers cutting
beef carcasses are smiling in
four quarter cuts,
and dressing carcasses and ribs
and plates, and chuck and shank.
The larger plants are equipped to kill many
hogs.
We're passing through this section.
The hair scraped from hogs and carcass is
dumped.
And there are more than a hundred different articles, from
kidneys to tongues and tripe.
There are casings for sausages.
There are by-products of seasoned meat,
and casings twisted into links.

There is a final examination
and a de-hairing machine.

The Spirit of Remembrance

I don't remember the agony, either.
I don't remember the first day of
school, I never heard the word "grades."

I went to the streets for my lunch.
I suddenly became an empty house,
a child wiping its eyes.
I feel something is so transparent in me.
I recite the 24 spaces of the spring day.
I am the spirit of remembrance,
of other children standing, observing.
I am the eyes of experience.
I am a kaleidoscope in the garden.
I am reciting to the class of junipers,
I sit on the couch of summer clouds,
and later, rejoin myself in the
very rudimentary song of wind.
I have never heard of the word "grades."
I erase grief.
I am the outdoor variety of joy.
I visit Edith and George in the garden.
Not wholly, I say, "thou shalt be in love."
I am beckoned to by the solstice.
I have suspicion that things will happen
just because I happen to be in the vicinity
of grace.

I might add that two girls are walking to the
arbor now, and before school is over,
and within fifteen minutes, and that is too soon,
I shall be right with the sun behind the
equinox, in the first chill of autumn,
with no feelings,
but your own.

Karen, Coming of Age in Ottawa, Ohio

Smaltz is in style. There she is playin' the
piccolo; it might be a hobby, a nice hobby,
next to the piano. She might be a member of the
Ridgewood High Band, but then again ...

Art Smith, who is the captain of the football team,
might change things.

There is a swimmin' date comin'.

Karen plays flute at the piano,
but there is a swimmin' date comin'.

Leave Ridgewood High.
get a swimmin' trophy.
Decorate some of your two hundred tunes.

Find what is angelic in a fur-lined fabric
with long legs.

The miracle of styling arrives,
and weightlessness, for smaltz is in style.

A long time fashion waitin' for you
at the piano,
and the clock ticks, the most important of places—
the clock.
No tones, no colours.
Look! The know how—

the long black coat of time.

The Angel Fish are Fifty Cents Each

There is a tropical wonderland in
Manhattan.

It calls for a special trip downtown,
to the thousands of rare and tropical fish

and exotic plants,
where several bunches of viscaria are background foliage.

I am a baby,
unappreciative of the practical problems involved
in areal plumbing.
I have my oohs and ahhs.
This is the first time I have made the trip
alone. I am looking especially for angel fish
and neon tetras.

I have acquired fifty little creatures of fluorescent
blue and
green for my river
room.

I see no violation of the stars.

And the dominating feature of the same shop—
heaven.
    (and the angel fish are fifty cents each)

Rain and the Afternoon

You're telling me?
I am a baby.
A funny one,
with a big broad smile,

and a waterfall tied to my back.
You're telling me what a
great thing a telephone is?

Just think.
If grandma hadn't seen me lose a tooth.
I'm one of the main reasons we have
telephones in the house.
You're telling me?
Mother has me tied down to a waterfall.

Suppose one of us got suddenly sick...

daddy doesn't cost much either.
I don't know, I don't know.

I wish I were a robber
and didn't worry about things when I
see a telephone.
I wish daddy couldn't talk to us when he's
out of town.

I'm in the order of things.
I can bet my life on it.

**Charlie Remembers that He
Has Been Here Most of his Life.**

The statues of Paul Bunyan and Babe,
the blue ox.
The legendary hero,
canoeing on the rivers and lakes,
the Minnesota wilds.
The quiet brook near Lake Itasca,
the ducks and many kinds of wildlife.

The millions of acres.
The thousands of vacationers.
The natural resources,
the Red River,
the lost deposits of granite,
the lumbering activities,

the plants, the blackberries, the lilies of the valley,
the raspberries, the rude anemones,
the wild geraniums.
The rivers, lakes and waterfalls.
The glaciers lying on many low hills.

Monique Arrives in New York

What is it that comes into view on the
broad horizon?
It is the new world, surprisingly comfortable.
It is the Statue of Liberty and the unabashed stop signs,
and the vitality, the little encounters that lead to
adventure. America comes into view on the broad horizon;
you can take it up as part of a holiday, as part of the Atlantic
between breakfast and dinner; it is the talk of passing people,
caught up in the tempo of exhiliration. Let me ask you
a personal question.
What is the temperature that enables you to grasp life without
fatigue?
America comes over the horizon in a city, in uninhibited talk.
It is the simple splendour of the age. It is easy to get there.
You set out to discover America. You are twice as alive as you were
before.
The spring may be rainy, and the winter bitterly cold, but
you will throw snowballs. You will live under a famed skyline.
You will walk with quick laughter, ready for more. You will find
interesting and beautiful friendships, for you are beckoned by
America on
the broad horizon, a civilized way of losing yourself, your arms
upraised in welcome. At night, you shall find everything pleasantly
possible.
You will find the man of your dreams. You will find him under a sky
bejeweled with lights, and people will talk to you, and remind
you how easy it is to be young, and part of what
streams around you, like love, and the crackling sparkle of life.

Mona; the Flower of Greenwich Village, Dying on New Years Eve

I am spending the day with old acquaintances,
and many such a day in memory.
I blithely watch the thirties go by me, and the
clarity of hangovers rebuke themselves. I remember the
interlude between labours, and the artists that were so
greedy, and the record of respective arts and unconventional
geniuses. I am remembering halleluiah, another New
Year and the many chronicles, and a man's touch that is
as delicate as a surgeon's. I have of many months late, of many
chronicles late been admitted to the well remembered
school days, and the wanderings that escaped poverty,
and what made merry. I am drunken snatches of joyous bands
of vagabonds, and grey leaves. I remember the odysseys of extravagance.
For many a day and many a night, I remember the small farms,
and the biographies of birch. I can't exactly see what is waiting for me,
but there is auld acquaintance, and the clarity of hangovers,
and the small farms, and the record of my halleluiah, when I am
punch drunk and turned into shocking thirst for the beginnings
and the end, for in full flower is my genius.
I consider the culture and the strata and the gusts of wind,
and turn at the turn of the year.

The Parson Walks Out into his Backyard Under the Moon

The power of faith

is a sign, is a girl living
in an abandoned village

is the organist not knowing
how to arrange for the invisible,

is a child enamoured of an image,
to reach the fourth and fifth rung,
to have the grasp of the joy of a cure.

That is a sign. The saints want us to stay alive,
and to live.

Parishioners refuse anything.
Miracles can be performed by a magician,
like a church that plays the organ and is
awakened to a child.

I am remembering how the full moon is
always swathed
in silvery light,
and is like a rare disease, like death,
united to my saintliness.

The Remember Widowing

I said, (I went on urgent in my argument)
I said, oh Ronnie, (and he laughed at my failure);
I said, my hand still remains in his,
and I cling desperately to it for reassurance.
I said, my face is the face of a very white
woman in search of a ghost.
And I won't say goodbye now, I won't
say goodbye though I expect everything, the
moon and the stars;
and I remember when Ronnie and I were radiantly happy;
we were happy throughout our wedding day.
And we hastily arranged for a carriage to come,
and fetch us,
and looking at him, I thought, I am amazed,
driving to the station, I am amazed that I
feel no urge to stay, huddling, and shivering
under a coat of stars.

The Man With No Heart

Who is the man with no heart?
Who is relaxing on the terrace with a refreshing
noon-day drink?
Whose words seem to jump out of his mouth,
and begin to attain serene perfection?
Who is the man relaxing on the terrace, thinking of
expanding his lawn, to include forty feet of
transplanted trees?

He is certain to hate, though he
loves his beautiful country home, with a
formidable batch of circulars and financial statements,
and a sigh of contentment.

The words seem to jump out of his mouth, as from
a page.
It is a dream finally come true.
"Mr. Sparling, in settling the estate of my aunt,
I want to make a generous offer of a wide swimming hole."

No heart. No heart.
He might be a sharp fellow, to everyone's annoyance,
but he won't be saddled with impossible situations;

a perfect home, bordered by a brook that doesn't
belong to him.

In the early evening he puts on his walking shoes.
It is the famous spring, clear and unutterably beautiful.

Look. What would he be willing to give away?
How foolish could you get?
I'll phone you, he says, and on the sixth day he doesn't phone.

Who is the man with no heart?
Kids are spreading it all over town.
He has only himself to thank. He stands out on the terrace.
He loves here more than he did in any other place.

He hears a noisy bunch of kids,
and the angels squarely on his side.

Almanac

In autumn, now in autumn, now in
late September, the strange and restless month,
the brightest and saddest month of the year.
Clear cool nights and sharp frosts, great quantities of
apples. It is apple picking time. The kids fill their burlap sacks,
and the apples sweeten, and darkness is outside the church door,
talking crops, talking the wood-box filled; now in
autumn is the time to dig potatoes, to watch the mice move
into the attic, the heavy jars carried to the cellar.
Tired men and women, squeezing into their narrow lives,
by the monotone and spell of autumn.

1956, A Year of Promise

1956, a year of promise,
as the old year closes through
fathomless vaults of time, and
tomorrow looms somewhere, in
a portfolio of photographs, I am the
portent of the future.
The nation has a heart-beat and
it throbs.
How can I recreate the earth's wealth and
the rich and amazing diversity that is
America?
How shall I gorge myself on the automobile?
How shall I find myself in a sea of golden grain?
These are my questions, unanswered.
This is my Everest.
This is man enslaved to the atom.

This is what can never be solved or understood—
the enigma of life and death, the rhythm of the
galaxy, the strong winds.

I can move swifter than sound.
I am the spirit of 1956.
I ponder where the trail leads.

I am unknown to scale.
I am a probe in interstellar space.
I am millions of my fellow man.
I am swifter than sound.

I am a thrilling pageant
and am not bewildered by the problems
on my own doorstep.

I will smash the matrix of yesterday.

The New Start

I shall say
come with me, and don't ask
what makes a manhattan; come
with me and vacation in Washington State.
Come with me to a
totally different world, a totally
different world—we'll go West. We'll
see how easily we can get around and enjoy
the thrilling sights of one thing after another—
the world in size and full of colour. Let us
go to friendly Washington State; the idea
is to seat you where you can blow
bubbles at the negative of the universe,
a unique picture.

Come with me to the Grand Coulee Dam, and
and let us make a masterpiece, the moment we set foot in
Washington State. The masterpiece of you and I, with
not more or less vermouth, but with a home for good,
with no strangers and no panic,
but with a home for good,
and the wonder of needing each other.

Sally Wonders in New Haven While Jack Boards the 6:15 on the Manhattan Line

This is my perfect house.
This is my fabulous house of the future.
The entire yard is stars, and
it makes for breakdowns in grief.

This is my fabulous house of the future.
It is a wonder, clear as running water.
It has a greenhouse and floors and walls
that are night sky, with simplified principles,
and food that can be stored like the good things
I have done.
Outside, the entire yard is littered with stars.

With every interesting feature
my eyes light up;
the year-round warmth of the air,
the sound of children whose parents are indifferent to
far away places.
Because nothing can be hurt here.

There is no work here and it is not a model home.
It is quite futuristic,
and eliminating of grief, and I will never tire of
living here.
I will always be able to change my needs,
and make room,
sandwiched between galaxies and stars.

What is Perfect About the American woman

As a Frenchman. Don't you think that in comparison ...
oh lacking the strong tradition of chic (how happy
she would be).

  Which brings us to
    the problem of makeup.
A friend of ours, editor of a
French women's magazine, buys all her shoes in
this country.

Then she made another lightning appearance.

Where does the idea of the unhappy, worried,
miserable American woman come from?
She is superb.

Any dictionary will tell you.

In the last analysis,
she is the backbone of the free world.

These Princesses

These princesses have all the variety and colour of gardens,
and become wood walkers and leaf watchers. There are so many
princesses in this world, any country man can tell you, the weather
conditions don't depend on it, it simply wastes away. The princesses
disintegrating, changing like spectacle, displaying leaves and
responding to ever deepening hues, the cool evening hues.

What are the right conditions for a princess at the
height of her brilliance? To be a golden leaf, to be dependent on
weather, to be part of the spectrum of pale gold in which
sugar remains, her happiness wanting to turn to deep blue?

The sadness of the princess is summer long, like
litmus paper.

One salvo before the continuous display
       of autumn.

Forget-me-nots

Villainesses, dark and slinky,
heroines fair and clean-limbed;
personalities instantly rewarded;

five foot eight,
tall, and weighing
a hundred and five pounds.

You tell yourself she is the most elegant woman in the world.
Luxuriant furs,
reminiscent of Garbo;
a smouldering tigress expression.

Separated from her husband,
she has had her fill of chic clothes.
She likes those comfortable casuals of leisure.

She goes to the theatre
in a sweater, a skirt
a raincoat.

    *

It's no accident.
It's no accident.
She likes to swim and ski.

She likes to commute to New York,

and enjoys country life.
She poses outdoors,
and her outdoor work features
sportswear and bathing suits.

"I'm not tall enough,
but I have a face for it."

While commuting
and while waiting,
she plans,

until her children come home.

    *

Sally Barfield is a veteran in the youth field.

She is in great demand as a "Junior" with
the big brown eyes, and loves
Junior sittings;

but she is too old for Juniors.
She is too old to be raising a family.

Is there anything nicer?
Is there anything nicer?

I depend on pretty surfaces,
and am brought
down to earth

by three sisters and two brothers.

    *

Here is Glenda McHenry,
Glenda McHenry, the last minute
replacement,

the girl with "bird-legs."
The editors call her "classic."
Glenda with her weakness in the
ankles.
Glenda of whimsy,
with a figure like a pop bottle,

and she flexes advertisements.

I pose. I have varicose veins,
I am alright.

⭐

Grateful to be with beauty photographers,
grateful to be with Trafari Jewelry,
I am the smallest model in the business,
with the round face of adolescence.
With a real attitude, high cheek bones
and a sense of balance,
and married at Teaneck, New Jersey.

I was your childhood sweetheart,
Mary Lou, Mary Lou Farnheim.

Mary Lou with the unhurried air,
Mary Lou with three strapping sons and
a Greenwich Village apartment.

Each picture goes on a page that says

turn.

The Dashing Newsmen of Paris March on a Blue Cloud:

We'll peep at one princess,
then another;
there are gates for a
hot scoop.
There is a papal servant, magnificently outfitted;
let us circle for a closer look.

They are consecrating new cardinals in a majestic
ceremony.
We are cheerful servants.
We are whisked away.
We are gate-crashing.

There are record players that blare jazz
all day,
and poodles that roam the bars.

Barefoot, we choose between sixty or so
pictures we will use.
Almost, exclusively, for a month,
we cha-cha to the Royal Ball.

In a reckless pursuit of news, we
have lost our lives.
We are a dashing blend of imagination
and courage, and brashness and the
world is full of innumerable scoops.
There are squads of police cars.
There is a stroll down the Champs d'Elysse.

Where is the greatest wonder?
The visitor between galaxies,
the daredevil photographers,
the Vatican officials,
the unique, unique picture with a
circulation of two million.

Where is the secret consecration?

chorus:

The greatest wonder of all is produced by all.
We spend most of the time playing poker,
throwing darts.

We don't believe in anything;
we are being viewed by millions,
splashed in vivid colour.

Within a week, the spectacular pictures
will reach Mars.
What is reality?

What does a parachute cost?
What is one village?
Who was the teenage hero of the
French Resistence?

We announce haughtily
"Philippe Petain, Maréchal de France."

Jeremy on His Fourth Summer Cruise

Even after day-long wear, the coat
still looks fresh. This is important.
It is important to be beautifully lined in
satin,
to be handsome,
to look well,
to have cuffs;

it is important to have a Bermuda holiday,
to stay at the swank castle,
to have days ablaze with sunlight,
and guidebooks and warm clothes,
to walk along the beach.

It is important to have a casual wrap,
and to travel Bermuda style, by carriage.

The coat and I.
The coat and I.

I am a copywriter's dream.
I move about the deck of the ship
on a Sunday afternoon. Perfumes. Woolens.

The islands are lush.
There are royal princes.

There is breath,
and stiff breezes.

And by night, there are the ocean tortoises.

Fanny of Omaha Wins a Trip

This is sunshine cruising, this is
the one holiday that everyone has promised you.
There are diamonds for you and breakfast in bed,
and chocolate and silken sheets and hours like this,
when Rip knows the Captain well and introduces you to
everyone on the ship.
Who would take this ride with anyone but you,
for you are the gayest of gay times, the quietest of
quiet times, the cuckoo is singing on the deck, announcing,
don't dramatize, wake up and see the whole
world as yours; the whole world as one place that has everything.

Don't dramatize, here's your little cabin, with diamonds for you,
and why not? You deserve it.
This is the delicious warmth of the Mediterranean sun,
far from the Sherman Oaks area. Dream of the bric-a-brac,
dream for the rest of your years,
dream far away from the street.
Release the fire imprisoned in your heart.

The Year of Promise

What does the year of promise hold for us?
Two thousand years after the Sermon on the Mount.
Decency and bursting vitality, exuberance.
All men are created equal,
washes to the shore for us.
Shall we see more than a measure of ignorance?
Shall we see despair replaced by hope?
A child plays at bearing witness,
and reminds us we all began in innocence.
Whatever happened to the dark passions that
rend men, remote as the alchemist's stone?

We are not bewildered.
Mind and spirit wrestle in the clouds, in this
brave new world of surf-bathing, amusement parks,
and aqua shows.
Where is the thin edge of the presence,
the galaxies that are helpless?

We solve, we understand
the amazing diversity that is America, 1956.
We will harness all the might we can create.
We will have no sad sacks.
Each moment is rich with portents of the future.
We are the town that refused to die.
We watch men's styles in clothing change slowly
and subtly.
Millions of dollars are saved every year.

We will keep this golden future for ourselves,
and the symbols of America, the
changeless beauty of the face,
and the forms so worshipped,
and God and religious faith,
and it is not strange to seek a deeper,
rapturous kinship, to soar toward the Almighty;
the largesse,
the variety,
the miracle of rain.

What is Tough for Children

What is tough for children?
The clash of personalities or the
furnishings of a very specific family?
The emphasis on burnt orange, and the
curves that give a dramatic splash to the settee?
What is it that's tough for children, besides being
foiled by the orange and pull-out bunk beds, and the
chest of drawers that take clothes and books?
What is tough for children? Welcoming the guests?
The new angle of living designed to make
children grow up faster? Living as a family can't be easy,
on an afrormosia floor, left uncovered, so that the
neighbours think the place is spotless.

No visitor identifies himself sufficiently,
to give a child an impression of a warm and beautiful house.

What is it that is tough on children?
Flowers? Shelves? Tables and chests of drawers?
A staircase, a bannister in a sleeve, a live-lime green
carpet?
What is tough on children who want to be light
on their toes before well illuminated mirrors, to
prance up to their bedrooms, looking for toys,
looking for little girls, of course, looking for
the patterns of foliage that make for
cheerful and sun-bathed mornings?

At Home

Here is a twilight view from the back garden; here is the
v-shape of the house; here is the interior view that shows
large living-dining areas and windows and prevailing West winds—
fixed windows facing North and East; here is the
magnificent view; I'll show you the angle of the v-shaped house.
The front has few windows; the fireplace is of pumice block.
The sky looks like a pale yellow ceiling.
      The living-dining area is at the right. The screen patio
in the centre. The twilight view from the back garden shows you
everything, and yet from a different direction comes the
waft of the citrus groves, from the mountains.
      Our answer is that the climate has been overcome.

The sky has a pale yellow ceiling,
as if it were all nearly under glass.

Proposal

Cool as a sea breeze, with sweeping curves and
floating colours, and a Mediterranean kitchen, a graceful snack
bar arc; past present and future blend. Futurama! Futurama!
Things rotate at a fingertip touch. Materials in
natural shapes and colours and textures. Impact. Circular
rosewood, a wheel on wheel work area.
This is my kitchen.
Here it is, my lovely kitchen. Curved appliance storage.
Homes! Homes! With a room like this, I create an
intimate garden area, no matter what the size of my world.
This is my bright area room, built in a summer house,
with fibreglass and insect screening, and a breezeway
between the screened room and the house.
Portal to portal protection, creates a blessing,
a pleasant visual blessing,
and look what the flowers can do, from sun-sweet golds
to burnished oranges, pink through ringing red,
blue mauves to sea-toned sapphires;

a muted background for a bachelor,
with added accents and original tones,

and you, in the background, would give a magic
arrangement.

Wherever placed, marry me.

Add sparkle and grace to my life.

Things I Still Want

The rich beauty of Pontiac's striking
Vogue Two-toning.

The Astro Dome dining car on
The City of Los Angeles Domeliner.

Panoramic sight seeing through six-foot picture windows.

Dude ranches in the wide open spaces ...

Nights ashore in exotic ports.
Old buildings near modern shops in Buenos Aires.

The Bel Air Sport Coupe with body by Fisher.

A Betty Crocker Chiffon Cake.

A pleasant Pullman lounge with fluorescent lighting
and big picture windows.

The Solar Lounge living room of the
New Moon Trailer.

Mobile homes at Solana y Sombra.

Riding the Vista Dome California Zephyr.

The Mount Vernon TV, with giant 19 inch, direct-view
Lifetone picture with a built-in FM radio, and plug-in for record
player.

The Strato-Streak V-8 power
of Pontiac's luxury ride and years of smooth
performance.

The new Dial-O-Map feature on
the Zenith Trans-Oceanic Radio.

The thistledown softness of Glide-Ride front
suspension.

To be amazed at the constant interplay between modern-age
convenience and the exotic customs and lore of
age-old origins.

Oldsmobile's F-85's exclusive Rockette Engine.

Christmas ornaments and textiles made of
polyester resin.

A two-toned Rocket 88 from Oldsmobile.

The radical new Turbo-Thrust V8,
agile and eager once you take the wheel.

A jet smooth Chevrolet
with the heart of one's serenity.

Vista Dome

How shall I see my way
to the Vista Dome, on the North Coast,
the Vista Dome, traveling through Chicago,
and the twin cities. How shall I arrive in
the deep blue American sky,
seeing the panavistas of America,
the traveler's rest buffet lounge,
the children's souvenirs; I yearn to see the
Pacific, from the Vista Dome. Here is a sentiment.
The Vista Dome.
Is there any reason to take seriously,
any and all the pitfalls of my life?

Mrs. Cox was persuaded to weep,
but I want to say to her "Come with me to the
Pacific's Vista Dome. It doesn't matter where
Dick is, it doesn't matter where Rodine Kansas is,
it doesn't matter where anything is.

Come with me."

Some Birds Go Southwest

Some birds go Southwest, to El Paso maybe?
Some birds do, and explore the sun everyday; Big Bend,
White Sands, Rio Grande. They see bullfights and rodeos
and picturesque and colourful snapshots. Some of the birds
are smart and go Southwest, where they will find friendly,
hospitable people. They are so lucky. They are so much in love to
see and do what the land invites,
as they fly happily—the smart birds that go Southwest—to
White Sands and Big Bend, and old missions, and enjoying the
high dry warm climate. The birds.
Do you know the birds add nothing to winter? The birds explore the
sun every day.

Their names shrink.
Their names are two million plus.
They wait for no winter.
They flap for a real change
and travel hard to be happy.

Desert Voice

I am only my own way to look for a place to hide,
and underneath the island palaces, the
decorated warehouses, the themes offering things
that preoccupy thoughts, I am a sleeping beauty, and
a Lilliput and the cues that telegraph Valhalla.

I am the Thunderbird and the Desert Inn with the
cabanas edged by the pool in the cinder block structures.
I am the Club Bingo and the Freemont's old West,
I am redwood used throughout the interior of concrete snakes,
and the architecture made for visibility that adds warmth to
the desert,
and in no way interrupts the view of landscaped gardens,
and the rooms of sky.
Beyond the rooms of sky are the open deserts,
crossed by the flora and asphalt roads and the
leafless telephone poles.

I am a roadside bandit, outlined in neon lighting,
the palette shaped for heaven,
the Five Strips resorts,
the assembly of glittering chrome at the north end
of the sky.

I am the spirit of Las Vegas, the Stardust, the
old West scenes, the neighboring Nevada,
the Mint, the Sands, the Dunes. C'mon and
compare the aristocratic scenes and spas of Europe;
feel my single strong formal gestures,
my curved facades, my chrome-clad frames,
and all my seven pleasure domes.
I am the spirit of Vegas,
with a panoramic view, and a casual ramble of
motel resorts, the Kachina Doll Ranch, the
rugged mountains that capture the shape of experience.
I am tapped into money, a gangster vision of heaven.
Look how the desert laps back at the doors,
and my broad roofs.

Pull back for an aerial view.

I am sad.
I am a figment.
Show me the ultimate reason for anything.
I weep beyond the Ramona Room in the main lobby.

California Zephyr

The California Zephyr.
It is streamlined and will go wherever you want it to go,
into a desert sunset,
into San Francisco,
among the mountain peaks.
It is lunchtime in the Rockies, aboard the
California Zephyr, and there's a desert sunset for dessert.
You are free, you are gazing one morning, you are
climbing the eastern slope of the Colorado Rockies.
You have put aside everything that grieved you.
You are riding to San Francisco, in the lounge car of
the California Zephyr. There's a buttery rainbow, there's a way
to see the world, moving to the upper reaches of the Feather River
Canyon,

lost
to grief and effaced momentarily, you take your first bite of
morning. The modern hype aside,
you are on the silvered streamliner,
far from the reaches of grief, far from the
features of death, far, far
and close, you are awake to yourself,
unsold, at last.

The California Zephyr
is streamlined and will go wherever you want it to go,
into a desert sunset, into San Francisco, among the
mountain peaks. It is lunch time in the Rockies,
aboard the California Zephyr, and there's a desert sunset for
dessert.

You want to know everything.
You want to be world famous in happiness,
and to remember, just to remember, all the scenery there is,
over and over again,
for fun, to be a guest in happiness.

I Promise You This

These are the exotic streets of many wonders,
the many exotic streets of America, unique America,
with teeming islands of bohemianism and modernism.
There's food for thought, there's St. Mary's Church, there's
Grant St. beginning, a high fashion market and Maiden Lane,
where dwell the fancy ladies and thirty thousand inhabitants,
where Chinatown is the second biggest in the country.
Oh, the oriental backdrop, the Golden Gate, the Grand Avenue flanks,
and Telegraph Hill, and what is America, unique among it's
tributaries and Croft St. and byways such as Noble's Alley and
and nests of sin, and temple bars, and musics, genteel and
properly liquid musics, and the atonal tinkle of a Chinese
butterfly harp, and a brilliantly lit shop that's swank, and we
walk a translucent sidewalk, and grin and
share it.

Taking an afternoon drive on the coast

I am fascinated by El Pueblo Del Nuestra Señora.
The town of our lady along the Pacific beaches,
that our Spanish forefathers named; beaches wide
and big, and the ultra-modern highway, skirting
along the coast, with the camellias and the azaleas
stacked in the sunny garden cafes. Beneath the snowy peaks
I can drive along the city limits modern as her freeways,
and lose myself among the ghosts of early padres.

Moving to California

The ideal city, I live in the ideal city so deep
in the balmy climate, under pagodas and pastel office buildings;
I live in the ideal city, so unmistakably Western, with
poinsettias and perpetual sunshine. And I am happy, on the
beaches, with the lush orange groves, and the valleys that
are so alive, the big colour map in my mind, the big colour
map with two summery deserts, lush deserts.
Do you know I live in an ideal city, in a town
that grows in my heart, that grows like the City of Angels?
The city of TV and radio stars.
I lose myself among the urban highways, with the wild
breeze of the South Seas, and the street names of America,
where I could easily spend my life.

Hooray for Hollywood

I Worship You

I worship you. The weeds move slightly.
They move their heads. There is, in the grass,
a small girl. Maybe she is a god, maybe she is a tribe,
maybe she is a great golden bird.

I worship you.
A troop of Indians appears, wavin' their spears, wildly.
What is a golden bird if not the one I love?

What is a golden bird if not a cry, a rock pointing to
a hollow place near the plain.

I don't suppose any of us will find out who we are.
But I worship you.

All of a sudden I turn around and become someone.
I look into your eyes, the weeds move slightly.

For all I know you are my chapter one.
Maybe you are a god. Maybe you're a little girl.

There is a nest outside, lodged just outside the window,
and some bird is bound to land there.

Once upon a time my mother was poor,
the chauffeur was poor, the maid was poor,
the gardener was poor.

That's how bird life goes.
Real life is sometimes different,

and that's Hollywood's contribution.

Bobby Kitonin Clears his Throat Before announcing the Hollywood Bowl Concerts on KJMT Los Angeles.

These are the starlight encores,
in the splendour of an outdoor setting
with music that gains a special beauty,
under the direction of Nelson Darnell, of
the Hollywood Bowl, on a starlit evening,
in the satire of mythology, in the spirit of
the world, with an audience fortunate enough
to be seen in the season's favourite musical
compositions, in the amphitheatre, with the
great artists and the wonderful spell, and the
charm of a starlit evening, in a summer evening,
with an orchestra, and the beauty that inspires, what
is most happily reflected in thirty seasons, following
a superb tradition of echoes and delightful spectacle,
and irreverence and the tremendous success of the elms.

Springtime in Hollywood

Springtime in Hollywood USA has a special meaning.
Crimson chested robins hurtling forth melodies,
flowers popping with their song, from their snug
winter sleep to make things look right; there are
warm breezes and green grasses, and star citizens

in a city delighted by what springs up along the
Sunset Strip—a breakfast of cornflakes, and baby ranches
and fashion settings and spotlights.
Look at Esther Williams and her sun-drenched backyard,
and the outdoor birthday parties and the celebrity children
with their ice cream headaches, and the yearning to be
in strange sounding places, far away places with
something new. The homes spring up along Sunset Strip;
forsaking Palm Springs for the seashore, we
are scanning travel folders, and warm breezes and
green grasses, to the cheery melody of 1955.

The Jet Revolution

All agree that the jet revolution
is six hundred miles per hour
with tape recorded music, and Californians and Europeans,
to Dallas and Boston and Miami, with Captain Eddie
Rickenbacker, to Central America and the Caribbean,
talkin' and readin' and writin' and sleepin'.
What are the predictions?
All agree that the jet revolution of the 1950's make
a forecast look like a science fiction magazine;
forty-five minutes from Los Angeles to San Diego.
Never mind four or five bus loads of passengers.
Within the cabin, about the width of a soft melody
you are arriving between time differences by
half the clock.
It means Hawaiian weekends! And no spot on earth
will be too far from you.
Check the background of the flight. It can happen
today, or tomorrow; no stress. Just the same sense
of movement as you feel sittin' in your living room with
a couple of evenings curled up. I am between flights.
I am your wake.
I am your concept of time across the face of the globe.
Get used to me; the blast of engines. I will deliver
you to America.
After your take-off, you will have to get used to the idea of
life, coast to coast, shrinking the earth, towed away by
runways, in the effect of the world's living.
The pure jet will wind up and mach up your time.

It is travel, 1955.
You have a cruising altitude and a distillation of moods,
and everything that follows World War II will be
magnificent.

The First American Man
Flies Over History and Spies a Hollywood Set

There is culture and history.
Pshaw!
There are the Apaches diablo and
and Eschamindians, and the Cochise.
There is the Sundance Kid
and an army of five thousand, established to contain
33,000 acres;
the prairies and the great plains are beautiful,
and the Montana desert, and the
California prospectors and the fortresses that
we put up. Who was the sheep-herding for, what
was the Alamo for, why was the
train figured to be the first and the last shot
in the smoke-belchin' hills?

Women, on the other hand are a disadvantaged
group.
They wither away in the traditional audiences of
cacti.
On the whole,
there are major historical themes starring
Tom Mix and others.
Not that historical references are
uncommon to women.
There are weightier themes.
There are immigrant trains.

There is Hoot Gibson who,
by contrast,
laughs himself to death with a minimum of action.

The Man Who Played Cochise

The phrase "like a phantom" occurs so often;
that's a big problem, to be depressed, not to be able to
argue with yourself in Buffalo, with fifty thousand young
women comin' out to see ya. The phrase "like a phantom"
has occurred so often. He stands a rugged six foot three,
a bachelor today, on the surface, but easy-goin', a noble
Indian you might say, a "blood-brother" a "Cochise" of
"Broken Arrow."
Black eyes; his eyes are brown; the big problem now is
casual moodiness. Deep problems? Forget it.
What do you want for *Cochise?* The first non-Indian ever
to be elected; he has a cupid's dart for feminine viewers,
but he gets depressed occasionally. He gets depressed.
He stands a rugged six foot three, and gets
depressed occasionally.
I think now that behind me is a rip-roarin' season.
And look at all the pale-faced maidens, Mr. Inscrutable,
Mr. Man-of-Many-Moods, both grave and gay,
with truckloads of mail, born a bachelor today,
of depression and loneliness.

Tempo 57, Or the Man Who Watched Too Much TV

Oh how sweet.
Do you really have the soft eyes I see?
Are they shared by millions of Americans on TV?
Mrs. Joe Buell, nationally famous home-decorating authority,
I find you longingly.
I want you.
I have always wanted you.
I find myself looking at you,
demonstrating that no home
is a dreary compromise when you
are in it.

Tempo 57.
I have a long-standing desire for you,
like a fox who hunts.
I am the male underground,
looking for the secret of Mrs. Joe Buell.
I have always carried forbidding topics.
I defend myself in a fancy dream.

I want to see the world with you.
I want to fall asleep, nearly exhausted in your arms.
Ordinarily—your crystal gazer, in a land without women,
like a fortune in a bottle, I translate and am
dressed for you.

Hollywood Hairdresser

I have the largest collection of movie star
photos in the world; Ann Southern, Bing Crosby,
Lucille Ball. I have Stoney Burke, and Jack Lord,
and Shelley Fabares, and in general my head is
swimming with the hit parade, with the
star parade, with two possible solutions,
and what can you do about it. I neither
smoke nor drink, and a funny thing happens to me
on the way to the lobby; "won't you," says the
woman, "come in and talk, so we can get acquainted,"
but I take only two kinds of customers, and they look like
Jackie Kennedy and Debbie Reynolds.

So,
you wanna see my largest collection of
movie star photographs in the world?
Dream. Your choice. Early baby Shirley Temple?
Or Richard Chamberlain.
All day, all night,
round the clock.
No aquamarine eyes for you; three shades—
jet black, rich brown, light brown.
How many applications of the stars shine
on you?

We are the funniest things, that make
a common sense to the popular explosions
of time.

The Notion of Envy at Paramount's Canadian News

In the upper room, newsreels from all over the
world, newsreels from all over the
world are in Paramount's Canadian news,

in sound track. What a success we've made of things
unanimous in choice, with the voice of *Wing Baron,*
a man already on the Paramount staff. Every Sunday night
radar, aerodynamics, and situation, flood the air waves,
and the sound of all the places we've never been to.

Foreign desks have been quietened. Museums are checked for pronunciation,
especially foreign pronunciation.
What is it we find traveling around the country meeting
editors and contacts, hob-nobbing with the stars?

Many a time, we've had a privileged look at everything.
But no, the old brain is still working, is still dreaming.
Often we treat ourselves, take ourselves around the country
to meet Yvonne Decarlo,

always alert to something extra.

Where is Morocco?
Where is the road to Mandalay?

Hollywood costumes
and the hand of *Baron* in the background.

What a chap! He arranges for everything.
Even the idea of stories.

Jack Parr

Find me a talent for tonight! I'm still tryin' to be polite, Tom. No Time's Square show-offs, no kids under eighteen, please, I thought I was rather definite about that. "Forget it" he says. "A couple o' bad notes won't matter." Well, what about Gleason's pants? What about the radio jobs and the customers that substituted for Jack Benny. Never mind Lindy's loitering comedian. We're lookin' at the young people, we're lookin' at the Jack Parr show.

Tom sums it up:
"this is amateur night." A young performer debating whether
to go to New York or not. Unless you have some contact established,
look at the necessities; the initiation fee is over a hundred dollars,
a singer needs to make the arrangements,
a boy needs a couple o' good suits.
The agent worries.

I can't understand it! For song and a dance?
Each has a fine voice and approaches the audition with
eagerness. Pride is the advent of Times Squared time.
A sense of discovery falls over the sky.
We broadcast in June.
It's a sleep-robber of a business.
But even more importantly, we have to pay the
train fare, so we need to be skeptical, we need to be
skeptical, we need to have new stars
that rise.

The Sometimes Date

Kim Novak's behavior is incomprehensible
to undeveloped hearts,
to the handsome and rich, to the puppies that are
always surrounding her; she swings her legs, she itemizes the gifts,
she loves strong yellows, and she's not public property. What is
the pretty pink cloud that surrounds her? And talks of
summoning her?
What is the tragic of the magic that never lasts?
I love her, and her stormy weather.
She gets carried away, too easily, far too easily.
She loves because she has to. She loves because she has to, she
collects love, she says I love you—it is the magic that
is life, that exudes glamour before breakfast is served.

I pause to rub my fingers.
I am withered by the incapacitating frost. I am
strong and handsome and rich.
I want to be Kim's popular mythology,
but she says no, and her eyes change from
powder blue to emerald green, and then to topaz yellow.

The tragic of the magic that never lasts.

She plants her flag up on a peak.
Kim is dating despite the press uproar, despite the Kansas winter.

It is a beautiful morning and life is exciting.
She has an emotional mountain for satisfaction.

She comes down again, where we can all breathe.

Shelley Winters

What I remember is her telling
Johnny Carson, when he asked her if
she had children, that she "never has anything around
the house that eats," and her
marrying handsome Vittorio Gassman—
       she's goin' to Rome.
       she's gonna have a baby
         and star in three films
           lucky thing, lucky thing.

She makes a man draw a quick breath
sizzling between the teeth
       she is a honey-topped bride,
and buzzes and bounces ... she's a whizz-head
she's a pack of vitamins
       and I love her Roman duplex, it is so posh, better than Beverly
       Hills.
But it is full of boxes and crates—
       is she moving out, and away from Vittorio?
Ask, oh ask ...
       thank goodness some men are coming
and some girls too, to help unpack.

       There's no place to sit. Let's help Shelley unpack
or we'll have no place to sit.

I Am the Cheery Melody of 1955

I am the cheery melody of 1955;
Skirts Ahoy, Scaramouche, and rollicking
hits, and Billy Ekstine, and Warner Brothers,

and Abbott and Costello, and *Those Wedding Bells*
and the Five Glamour Ensembles.

I am the melody of 1955.
Looking lovely *With a Song in my Heart,*
and a fabulous cavalcade, and Miss Show
Business herself, *up a ladder of musical triumph*—

Susan Hayward;

say look Ava and Frank have put the redecorating touches on their Palm Springs home.
Have you got any idea of what to do with a ribbon?

(The anatomy award goes to Virginia Mayo).

What's in it for Miss America?

A seashore resort.
A carnival of beauty.
Crowded hotels and shops.
A $5,000 dollar scholarship.
Four advertising contributors.
One completely unofficial prize.

Some eager males.
Marriage proposals.
Bank balances and stock holdings.

Florida's Orange and Tangerine Bowls.
A fast plane.
The Florida Citrus Commission.
An extra large glass of orange juice.
Philco Playhouse television shows.
A black bathing suit.

Chaperones.
The end of a rainbow.
Income tax.

Her Agent

A double in shade, such a pretty girl, and then
a brunette. TV's demand for her is relentless;
the unbilled blonde!
Normally blonde, but the day's work done, she
pays off, beginning to look like a nation's grief.

Here she is and I am mighty masculine.
With her hair half blonde, and all brunette,
she pushes into the daily operation of two networks.
Blonde hair, she failed to reply to blonde hair.

Who is that fairy group's dance queen?
She is!
The unbilled blonde.

Move over. Both versions happen.

Give this note to the woman sitting alone

Oh sultry voiced songstress, well dressed,
lovely lady.
You are a song. You're a village and every town.
You are never discouraged, for you have
western gentlemen, your rapid rise to stardust.

After you took to tremendous trembling,
your typical pose was dream-come-true.
Get back to *Norma*, get back to the summer at Bala,
one foot in front of the other, and the waves,
the rapid rise of the tide, as you sank in the
beauty of your voice.

The Tonight Show

My true romance.
What is it that makes the difference between a
happier story and a train fare? Steve Allen knows.
Steve Allen grabs it. The ratings soar
over the show. We're looking at performers, lookin' to
find new acts, we're lookin' at Parr's
do-unto-others talent policy. We're talkin' a happier
story concerning a young man who states frankly
he
wants an audition.

Tom cringes at this approach.
"Right for Parr" says O'Malley.
The agent worries.
"When we feel someone is right for Parr,
we know it"!

Talking to his Manager

Information, Bob! The seven hills of Rome and acting
on the cuff; that's my style!
That's my playhouse. Charged with brutality?
It was just a little clash, that's all. And you wanna talk about

the Mutual Aid Society and a marriage before
Preston and Carol?
Please, give me some information! Please show me the
man from Laramie, Wyoming; any place will do, so long as
there's a chance of meeting with a Hollywood agent. Gabe is
supposed to show up. He's from Okotona, Minnesota, and they
don't come any smaller than that. Marshal has an apartment! And
he's been in New York already for a month with his beagle, Rusty.
I wanna explain my devotion. I wanna sing boy, sing. I wanna
have a touchstone in Manhattan, and model for a raft of dramas.
Information, Bob! I need information. I need a starring role with
the husky Clint Walker. I want a homespun tale of makin' it,
like the likeable kid in *Shane*. I want a sinister part in a fast-moving
western—distinguish myself.
I have learned a warm and gay romantic manner, faithfully,
for the Screen Actors Guild.
Peter lives in glamour!
I prefer to live without a story, without a musical family,
in daytime hours, and not as one of nine new men on the
Lawrence Welk team.

I am alert! More convincing than if I had found uranium.
I am eligible.
And I combine the pleasure
with no ordinary girl.

The Art Critic Dashes his Brains Against a Rock in Arches National Park, Utah

Walt Disney faces the camera and Bob Cummings,
for instance, is brooding over iffy reviews. There is
art-mindedness, there is art that is a one and only thing. There
is art that is derivative of art, and action
paintings so formulaic, so reticent in meaning,
and uniform, and what is the difference between a picture
hanging over the mantelpiece and one on the TV set?
It is the 1954–55 season.
New paint by numbers kits are flooding the country.
Maria Callas goes out with a troop of jugglers.
Everything is occupied in the same electronic frame.
To optimists, the lion's share of attention goes to a
do-it-yourself author of a record. We've tossed Van Gogh
into the depression era. There are pin-ups and tip-ups,
and art professionals and sidewalk art sales in New York.
What is a self-service art?

It is in a New Jersey supermarket
competing with boxes of detergent.

Sparky, the TV dog

From the top of the Belmont Hotel in
Miami Florida here I come,
after a hard day of cruisin'
automobiles and *bark-quik* dog biscuits.
I have a special funny bone quality about me, I am
an ad lib comic, I have a hydrogen bomb in my pocket,
and a melt-in-your-mouth *bark-quik* dog biscuit;
I am steaming, I am bitin' mailmen. I am irritable after a
hard day's work bitin' mailmen. Spruce me up! Spruce me up!

(I am shown here with Bob standing beside his wife, Lee Pepper.

Everyone is standin' except me.)

Bob and Ray, TV Comics and Back Taxes

Bob and Ray drink milk and have mustache cups,
counterfeit, you might say, thoroughly dry—
the name must begin with an "o," with a "y."
Win a seahorse! An authentic seahorse—
there's a seal of approval
and the best chocolates you've
ever had, mottled green plots,
red white and blue caps. A candy discovery! That's what
Bob and Ray have—is a candy discovery, all cream chocolate
squashed in the exact centre, bottom eye, top eye. Have
you ever opened a box of candy and pawed through it?
Pre-thumbed them?

Bob and Ray have moustache cups, and keep a
sharp eye out for the feds,
hangin' near the future.

Liberace

This sort of thing is no different from
all the others. Actually, Liberace is enough of
a musician to have appeared as a guest soloist
with the Chicago Symphony. He plugs his records,
winks at the crowd, typifies his finger work and ...
boom! back to Hollywood, thank you very much,
thank you, thank you very much, as he plays, smilin'
and winkin', flips up the tails of his dress suit. He
probably will be up before sunrise to fly to
another city, where bleats of rage will gain him more
newspaper space and purrs of approval. Peanuts,
soft drinks, records and photos on sale in the lobby.
A sweet young man playing a variety of shortened classics.
Now and then, he sings and digs up
clippings. He is a splendid appearance.
He travels with six musicians, and prattles on
like a nice small town boy.
But he wants to explain "there aren't any
birds in the grass,"
he wants to explain simple things,
like old time sentimental tunes, in an
agreeably nasal voice.
One night he returns from San Francisco
in the frost,
and meets himself in person.

So far as he knows his friendliness is a notable
part of his character.
He tells himself he has one reason for erasing memory,
and it has nothing to do with
six thousand women jammed into a hall.
It has to do with working perfectly,
every day, another day; the great spectacle,
the glamorous son of Wisconsin, wildly optimistic,
and stunned with experience,
another wide-eyed masterpiece of America.

After Losing His Wife to Insanity

Andy Williams country.
Well, there's a lot of walking and talking to do,
how the streets look at night, and those strolls.
Maybe we're talkin' East 90th St. and Madison Avenue,
and his dog Barnaby and tulips in red and white and
pink planted in long boxes on sidewalks. We'll talk about
a path that leads to the park that reminds him of
Iowa and the summers he spent there. We'll talk about
wandering near the docks late at night,
pondering the latest trip to Europe,
and how midnight thoughts hook up with
couples walking hand in hand.

Waking Thoughts of the Stars

Frank Sinatra

Tantrums.
The Chi Chi Club in Palm Springs.
Dancing with Ava.
A friendly hide-out.
An argument with Lawford.
Rancho Mirage.
Bottomless money.

Jo Stafford

Buddy Rich on drums.
The class beach party.
Bathing suits.
Sitting in corners.
Singing.
Grooming tricks.
A court bungalow.
A skinny Frank Sinatra.
Dates and faces.
La Martinique.
Going back to the beginning.
Being different.

Jackie Gleason

Soft music.
Sending a gift to Alice.
Soulful Romantic music.
Fifty one musicians.
A red plaid dinner jacket.
Dance numbers.
Hating lights.
A rooming house at Asbury Heights.
A man dressed as a bear.

Jack Lemon

A tiny Ford Thunderbird.
Sylvia and the Hollywood
Pantages Theatre.
Clark Gable stripped down to the waist.
New Hampshire school chums.
A seventh floor walk-up apartment.
Roses.
Lost furniture.
A Finnish housekeeper.
Lost furniture.
Dumbbells weighing thirty pounds each.
Water splashing over the yard.
The basement.
Guests.

Tony Curtis

My father's sideburns.
Peasant dresses from Hungary.
A brother dying.
Beauty in all things.
Gypsies.
Tipping a cab driver.
The time it snowed in Los Angeles
in 1949.
Two men who are dead.
Buying acreage on the moon.
Mixing blue with yellow.
Not finishing school.

Lauren Bacall

The age of 32.
Tragedy
The Santana.
Photographs of old friends.

Depth of feeling.
A town crowded by malign flatterers.
Ideas changing.
Each day being a little bit better.
Visitors not coming.

Kim Novak

Lavender floors.
Incapacitating frost.
Someone who is strong and handsome and rich.
Mountain peaks.
Violet eyes.
Moist tropical weather.
Bel-Air
Self-doubts.
A pink cloud of new love.
Driving down canyons.
Imported cognac.
A whirlpool of excitement.
Learning how to love.

Elizabeth Taylor

A wedding bouquet.
Hearing the voice of love each night.
Acapulco, scarlet flowers.
Newspaper clippings. A swim in the bay.
A proud wifely expression.
A villa on the Riviera.
Driving winding roads.
Exquisite furs.
15 river steamers, hundreds
of bottles of champagne.
Madison Square Gardens. Sight-seeing.
A fitting room.
Nightmare lights and heat.
A virus infection.
To be free of something.

Dick Clark

Cookies.
Five hours sleep.
Erasing temptation.
Oral communication.
Dance committees.
Water seeping in.
Pictures of outstanding students.
Money in a dish in the top drawer.
Picnics and crazy pictures.
Mowing lawns.
A harmonica. A little whisk broom.
A record collection.
Warm lasting friendships.
Going steady.
A suburban apartment.
A handful of bills.
A wedding band.
A philosophy of life.

Deborah Kerr

Numerous Hollywood parties.
Casually coming together in Vienna.
Children that can't sleep.
Church going.
Any small American town.
Weeping.
A city of dreams.
Restaurants lighted with candles.
Chestnut trees. Lilac bushes.
Mile upon mile of lilies in the valley.
Violets growing wild, scenting
the air.

Errol Flynn

A South of France evening.
The Hollywood dung-heap.
The owner of a local bar in Lone Pine.
The traffic of Pico Boulevard.
A memory full of beauty.
Reporters. Illegal cockfights.
A loaded revolver.
Minor ports of the Mediterranean.
A quay-side bistro.
A place of ghosts.

Douglas Fairbanks

A sad, over-furnished place.
A Santa Monica beach-house
A billowing main-sail.
Smartly-dressed guests.
Dead chickens impaled on stakes.
Love of youth.
A knife in the guts.

Danny Kaye

Off-screen faces.
Specialty numbers.
Children.
New cheesecake.
Borrowing a wig.
Louis Armstrong rehearsing a song.
Cat's whiskers.
The fun of living.
Going for a stroll in the skin.

The Moon and Frank Sinatra

The women I loved, the women I hated

and sadly only one side of the moon,

only one marriage, an aphrodisiac,
and over-sized bow ties.

There are plains and oceans and lakes and dry plains.

At ease with my remoteness, and capable of being
a friend, every day life and the major deeper themes.

The bay of dews, the sea of showers, the ocean of storms,
the sea of tranquility.

I remember a wedding planted with a bogus announcement,
being blind-sided at an intersection, and Jilly's Palm Springs Club;

the lake of the dead, the lake of sleepers, the sea of nectar,

I am ready to die on stage, world-bruised and idealistic;

the Moscow sea. I am so fed up with the jibes of the
New York Daily Mirror,

there is a beating for the bad press, a place in the sun,
and Jimmy, my shadow, the moon and the man, and

in rotation, only one side of the moon.

His Memory

Why do we forget?

So a singer loves the fighter legend,
what of it?
So I met Jimmy Dorsey in 1940,
and what is electrifying?

Lettuce, peas, tomatoes, apples and
pudding,
produce a failure of remembering.

A day, probably less, leans towards the
morning, and the first learning, and weeks later,
and the memory so connected, and the
individuals so forgetting.

I remember Capitol recordings, a shot glass,
I remember a stable of show girls,

and two items, just before going to bed,
memorizing teachers and psychologists,
and everyone remembers the many days,
how close a friend got, the White House, the
first hit, and the terrible death.

Recitation, recitation, the first to
reclaim an original life, and a person
who fully learns, and the second time faster
than the first time, to remember it well, and
quickly, and sometimes to recall.

To be finished, to take care of the kids, to not
be afraid of drowning.

The lyrics that loved the way I did, the voice,
the aria, the mood. To be married for
the lack of it;

for a person who can remember the entire list,
for a person aware of remembering anything.

Jack Parr Leaves the Network

I don't know what to tell you about the show,
the honest reaction of the audience, the same
purpose time after time. Bob Cummings came in,
with his oldest son, sat down at the front, and said
"can't even find a word for it." The shows they put on
film are run for live audiences and the engineers always
crack up. Let's leave it to a question of excellent tastes
and a gorgeous wife.
I love it!
I don't miss anything.
I mean my honest reaction is that
children should know what to do with their dads,
without all the vivid oil paintings and the coral couches,
and blends of contemporary oriental decor;

I am a reward of success.
A little tired, but a reward of success.
I mean, Gabriel, blow your horn.
I have just learned that a family surrounding me
is enough talent for one night.

Shangrila

The bird flies up from the branch, on its way, on
its way, on its way, flitting around the lights below the summit.
The bird is a mountaineer perhaps or is an unusual sight,
is on a climb on it's way to a tragedy, but the bird also
moves in the garden, where there are rescue teams in the
night, bringing the scents of azaleas and nightshade.
The tight rope dropping from the sky, there are nineteen climbers—
the bluebirds. Some of them will reach the summit, because
God is happy. The two in the middle sing, are not found dead
in the crevasse. They fly from pine branch to pine branch,
simultaneously inspired by a peasant or princess.
That's how birds are, Unmistakably,
hitherto rushing into a melodramatic ending,
the bluebell.

A Little Fat Man Rises from a Leather Chair in the Cartwright Wing of the Columbia Pictures Building, 1955.

In addition to freeing itself
of external pressures,
Hollywood needs to air its
own self-censorship, and come to
conclusions, run by major companies,

with specialized audiences.
We don't
intend to make concessions to anyone.

We don't intend to make concessions to anyone,
because we want to stay in business.

First, the motion picture is a medium
of entertainment.
It is a form of art.
It is a mass medium.

In view of these factors.
In view of these factors.

Yet the motion picture by no means
ignores the artistic.

Just walk out with what is wrong with it.

The great mass of people, so innately,
decent.

Acknowledgements

I'm grateful to those whose graciousness exceeded the call of the contemporary, among them:

David Belusci, Gianni Carparelli, George Elliott Clarke, Rita Davies, Denis De Klerck, Joey Delamarina, Barry Dempster, Bill and Jean Gairdner, Michael Henry, Isabella Colalillo-Kates, Al and Lorraine Kussin, Corrado Paina, Michael Redhill, Vaclav and Kristina Vaca, Olga Stein, Don Gorman, Francesco Loriggio, Wendy Woodworth, Harold Heft, Rudy and Muriel Sorrentino, Teresa Sorrentino, Tom Wayman, Kay Malenfant, Dino Patitucci, Domenico Pietropaolo, Rudy and Sandra Wietfeldt, George Williams. I owe a special debt of gratitude to Angela Gulia, who co-visioned this book, and to the many men and women who spoke to me in a love of time.